The Mind *for* His Glory

A PHILOSOPHY OF APPLIED
CHRISTIAN PSYCHIATRY

Adam O'Neill

The Mind for His Glory: A Philosophy of Applied Christian Psychiatry.

Independently Published: Fairfax, VA

Copyright © 2024 by Adam O'Neill

Front image: Adapted from Michelangelo [Fresco] *The Creation of Adam* (c. 1512). Public Domain. Design: Cover (front and back) and typesetting – Sarah Asaro

All rights reserved. No part of this book may be scanned, uploaded, reproduced, distributed, or transmitted in any form or by any means whatsoever without written permission from the author, except in the case of brief quotations embodied in critical articles and reviews.

Unless otherwise noted, scriptural references are taken from the English Standard Version.

ESV Study Bible: English Standard Version. Crossway Bibles; 2008.

In this book, all names, identifying details, and certain characteristics of individuals and cases have been changed to protect the privacy and confidentiality of patients. Any resemblance to real persons, living or deceased, is purely coincidental. The medical cases presented are based on real scenarios; however, modifications have been made to ensure anonymity and to adhere to ethical standards. This book is intended for educational and informational purposes only and should not be used as a substitute for professional medical advice, diagnosis, or treatment.

ISBN: 979-8-9870037-6-3 Printed in the United Staes of America.

The Mind *for* His Glory

DEDICATION

To my fellow workers in the Lord. May you be strengthened with power through His Spirit and to His glory.

Adam O'Neill

CONTENTS

	Author's Preface	i
	Introduction	v
1	To Provide Holistic Psychiatry and Mental Health Services	1
2	That Through Mental Wellness	33
3	Patients Will Grow in Their Knowledge of God	55
4	Be Conformed Into the Likeness of His Son	95
5	To Become More Effective for the Kingdom	117
6	To the Glory of God	139
	About the Author	159
	Endnotes	161

AUTHOR'S PREFACE

"It is a lame creature who calleth himself a physician and he be void of philosophy and know her not."

PARACELSUS

What comes to mind when you hear the words mental health? Perhaps you think of Simone Biles and her early departure from the 2021 Olympics to pursue therapy. Maybe the tragic death of Robin Williams to suicide. Or maybe you think of Dr. Phil and his guests storming off the stage in mixtures of fear or anger. Perhaps mental health reminds you of events closer to home; a family member comes to mind, and you recall their struggle with depression, all the things the doctors tried, some of the treatments that helped, and some that seemed to make things much worse.

What comes to mind when you hear the word psychiatry? Perhaps a patient on a chaise lounge and the occasional "how does that make you feel?" interrupting an otherwise stream-of-consciousness conversation. Maybe a darker image of straitjackets and electroconvulsive therapy, involuntary admissions, and forced medications?[1]

The answers to these questions are more than just a practice in free association; it's an exploration into the attitudes and beliefs of a field that has become more or less one of the most talked about areas of the human experience in our time.

Whether you think of meditation or medications, psychotherapy or pop psychology has a profound impact on how you will approach, receive, and, for those of us in practice, provide mental health care.

The Christian pursuing mental health is caught in an uncomfortable position. In America, there is a great risk for mental health to become an idol. Therapy styles, meditation, and medications have become, for some, the sole source of hope or healing and, thus, an object of worship. Christians are right to avoid this mentality. On the other hand, many in the church struggle with cognitive distortions, physiologic symptoms of depression and anxiety, addictions, and even psychosis, and wonder if there are things in psychology and medicine that might be used for their good in healing and to God's glory.

This book attempts to present one provider's approach to psychiatry as a Christian. Of all the specialties in medicine, psychiatry logically seems to be the one for which ethos and practice philosophy are most important. Christian philosophy is important for the cardiologist, pulmonologist, and even the radiologist as they care for humans impacted by the fall. Still, it is in the field of psychiatry that the worldview impacts not only the focus of an individual session but also its goals and outcomes.

In secular theory, psychiatrists often vacillate between maintaining a professional distance from their patients and attempting to adopt different worldviews to enhance therapeutic connections. The former is arrogant and cold, unhelpful in practice, and rarely possible (as having no worldview is itself a worldview). The latter, assuming the worldview of another, is an attempt at empathy. Still, only subpar advice comes from those who are partially invested in the particular "why" behind it all that represents a person's worldview. The issues we discuss are ones on which we stake the fate of our souls; you want your provider metaphorically on the same life raft as you.

Ideally, the patient and provider would share the same worldview, its strengths, joys, struggles, hardships, and pain. Viktor Frankl, in his *The Doctor and the Soul*, wrote, "The [practice of medicine and psychiatry] becomes equally easy for the doctor who happens to unite within himself the qualities of physician and religious person, and who discusses questions of belief or value with patients of his own faith."

In my first book, *The Mind After Eden: Psychiatry in a Post-Fall World*, I focused on theory and applied concepts with case studies from practice. This book will primarily include theory, though this is not because of a lack of clinical success in its application. In addition, the exclusion of many cases is because I believe theories should be evaluated based on their best application, something I do not claim to have mastered, though I progressively work towards. I hope that by writing down and publishing these principles, I can be held accountable by those who work with and for me. Additionally, I invite anyone in the field who believes these principles to approximate Truth to apply them individually and report on findings.

Anne Lamott said, "Almost all good writing begins with terrible first efforts. You need to start somewhere." I believe that is true. I also believe that all the best writing isn't final but is, in some ways, alive, clumsy, and filled with mistakes, not purposefully, but because the author is human, fallible, and fallen. The Bible is the only writing in which you can have confidence in its perfection. I ask you to read these pages first, graciously, then take them and edit them/notate them extensively. Compare these theories to the Truth of our gospel and read critically.

I pray that these pages are as edifying to you in reading as they were for me to write. We must remind ourselves regularly, lest we become discouraged, that one day, this book will no longer be needed, when pain will be replaced with pleasure, malady with magnificence, and disorder with design by our Good Creator and King, Jesus.

Until then.

The Mind for His Glory

Adam O'Neill

INTRODUCTION

"The life so short, the craft so long to learn."

HIPPOCRATES

If an archer were to set out to shoot an arrow from a bow, I should hope the most important part of the preparation would be to set the target. Ideal craftsmanship of the bow, a calibrated arrow, perfect form, the right weather conditions, and mindset all do no good if the arrow is fired opposite its intended target. I feel the same about psychology. Inasmuch as psychology has been defined as the study of the human mind and its functions, its implied target is that through this understanding and application of what is learned, humans may live in a state of mental health. As I propose in this book, mental health is not just the absence of pathology but the presence of a right orientation of the mind. Stated another way, mental health is not a neutral position, like a vehicle on idle, but a car driving to a destination. The psychologist Abraham Maslow, in his order of physical and emotional needs, placed "self-actualization" and "transcendence" at the top, showing that after all human's physical, emotional, and cognitive needs are met, the mind naturally turns to thoughts of one's purpose (how one might live into that purpose) and how that purpose relates to a need to devote oneself to something greater (and outside) oneself.[2] This is self-actualization and transcendence, respectively.

For Christians (and non-Christians, though they may not be aware of it), the grand unifying theory of human self-actualization and transcendence is clear: We are most authentically ourselves in glorifying God. In our blessings, trials, justification by faith alone, or eternal punishment and separation from God, our purpose is to glorify God.

We have the ultimate example of this from our Savior. It was the orientation of Christ's heart to glorify the Father in his darkest hour, "Now is my soul troubled. And what shall I say? 'Father, save me from this hour'? But for this purpose I have come to this hour. Father, glorify your name'. Then a voice came from heaven: 'I have glorified it, and I will glorify it again'" John 12:27-28.

This glorification of God is continued, magnified, and reciprocal in the relationship of the Trinity, who is ever being glorified and glorifying one another for eternity past, present, and future. Before Jesus' betrayal, arrest, and crucifixion, he offered the "High Priestly Prayer" for his disciples and all believers for all time. In this prayer, Jesus describes this reciprocal glorification present in the Trinity, "Father, the hour has come; glorify your Son that the Son may glorify you…" (John 17:1).

We enter into this relationship as well, "All mine are yours, and yours are mine, and I am glorified in them" (v10) and again, "The glory that you have given me I have given to them, that they may be one even as we are one... I desire that they also, whom you have given me, may be with me where I am to see my glory that you have given me because you loved me before the foundation of the world" (v22-23). Scripture instructs us to orient ourselves toward the glorification of God (see Matt. 5:16, Rom. 11:36, 1 Cor. 10:31, Eph. 1:14, Eph. 3:21, Phil.1:11, 1 Tim. 2:13, among many others).

From this, we derive the rightly oriented Christian psychology: you are never more authentically yourself, never more actualized, to use Maslow's terminology, than you are in the worshipful posture of glorifying God. One of the core tenets of Biblical Counseling is that we are all, by nature, worshipers of something.[3] A correctly oriented psyche realizes this worship's intended source, God. Original sin began in the pride of disordered worship of God and onto self.

The world, guided by this original sin, would have you believe that to be truly and authentically yourself, you must be everything but what makes us truly ourselves—the worship of a God that is not ourselves. Our fallen nature inclines us toward pride. But in worship of God by our words, actions, attitudes, and response to life circumstances, we take our rightful place and are authentically human, reassuming our position in complete subjection to his rule and reign in our lives.

In this view, Maslow's concepts of self-actualization and transcendence are not distinct. The greatest purpose you can live into as a "self" (self-actualization) is to realize your purpose exists in something outside the self (transcendence). This theory would impact every area of our lives. For example, self-actualization through child-rearing is not an end in itself, but that children may be brought up in the instruction of the Lord (Eph. 6:4). Excellence at work is not as if for earthly managers but for the Lord (Col. 3:23-24). Good nutrition and physical health are important because our bodies are a temple of the Holy Spirit and are made as image bearers of God (1 Cor. 6:19).

Given this, a book on the practice of psychiatry as a Christian is most accurate and authentic if it aligns with this target. This is how the mission statement of my practice was developed.

We exist…

(1) To provide holistic psychiatry and mental health services that (2) through mental wellness, (3) patients will grow in their knowledge of God, (4) be conformed into the likeness of His Son, (5) to become more effective for the Kingdom, (6) to the glory of God.

The chapters of this book are divided by the individual pieces of the mission statement. Each will be explored separately yet they interact with one another. As we grow in knowledge of God, we understand how He would have us live; this leads to conformity. The greater our conformity to Christlikeness, the more effective we become for His Kingdom's work here on the earth.

The use of medicine and psychology, which orient themselves around the isolation of a problem through accurate diagnosis and treatment and eventually reaching resolution, is not an ultimate end but one of the good gifts God has given us to further glorify Him. This relationship is displayed in Figure 1.

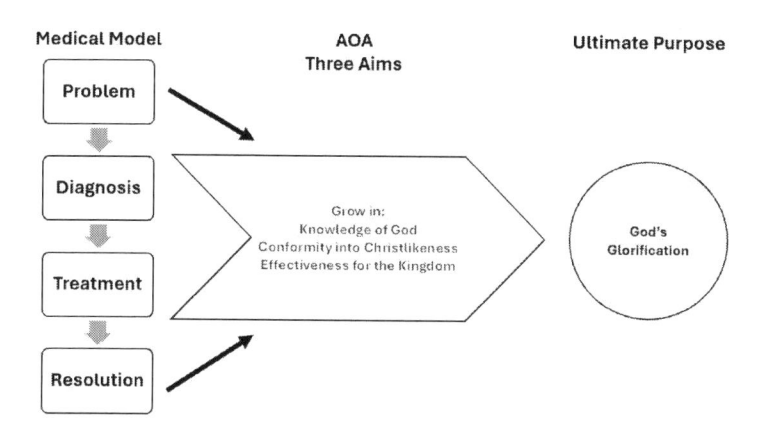

```
Medical Model              AOA              Ultimate Purpose
                        Three Aims
  Problem
     ↓
                      Grow in:
  Diagnosis           Knowledge of God
     ↓                Conformity into Christlikeness      God's
                      Effectiveness for the Kingdom    Glorification
  Treatment
     ↓
  Resolution
```

Figure 1. A proposed model of integrated Christian psychiatry. Three aims are those described for patients treated at Adam O'Neill & Associates (AOA).

Through these chapters, we will explore the field of psychiatry and mental health, the reasons for mental (as well as physical) maladies and what authentic mental wellness looks like, the importance of growing in the knowledge of God, the sanctification process of being made into the image of his Son, and realizing our role in God's grand plan—becoming more effective in our service to Him, to His glorification. In addition, we will identify those areas of secular medicine and psychology that may be viewed as good gifts of common grace and those that distract from our pursuit of God's glorification. Of these good gifts, St. Augustine writes, "If the things of this world delight you, praise God for them but turn your love away from them and give it to their Maker, so that in the things that please you you may not displease him."[4] Put briefly, it is about stewardship, not inclusion or exclusion. With the target identified, we metaphorically turn to the bow, the arrow, the training of the bowman, and all those other valuable skills that help us hit the mark swiftly and accurately.

CHAPTER 1

TO PROVIDE HOLISTIC PSYCHIATRY AND MENTAL HEALTH SERVICES...

"The good things which you love are all from God, but they are good and sweet only as long as they are used to do his will. They will rightly turn bitter if God is spurned and the things that come from him are wrongly loved."

ST. AUGUSTINE

In the first chapter, we must address, definitionally, several components before moving to the practical application of mental health to a patient. First, how do we define holistic? This necessitates a discussion on the nature of humans as both a physical body and an immaterial soul/spirit. Next, we will discuss what we call the mind, which is the chief target of psychology. We then discuss the application of secular medicine or psychology to both Christians and non-Christians. Finally, we discuss the pedagogy of training practitioners to offer these holistic services to patients.

The Dual Nature and Integrated Christian Psychiatry

On the main level of the science building at Wheaton College, where I studied as an undergraduate, swung a massive pendulum. Day and night, it moved back and forth, passing methodically between lighted indicators to show its rotation. As a testament to the God who created our world, our eyes were drawn upward by the long metal cord to the ceiling painted to appear as the sky with billowing white clouds and a light blue background. Between classes and before exams, the swinging metal pendulum stood as a silent testament to the ordered world we inhabit.

Above the main level was the chemistry floor, where beakers sloshed with liquid reagents, fume hoods where Bunsen burners flamed, and chemicals behaved in predictable ways when mixed. The walls were covered in diagrams of atoms and molecules, and the Periodic Table of Elements proudly displayed a testament to each element's organized nature.

Above chemistry was physics, where whiteboards stood covered with more letters and symbols than numbers for comfort, and further up still stood the floor that connected to the roof by way of an enormous telescope housed in its observatory. Late on clear nights, I joined my astronomy colleagues in looking at monitors that received images from deep into space. Here, as if to match the pendulum below, our eyes were drawn upward, further than our natural vision allows to the unseen world of celestial bodies. Jupiter, its great spot; Saturn and its rings; and Mars, our closest neighbor. Further out still other stars and galaxies of sizes incomprehensible. These are also governed by the laws of physics and nature.

Massive yet predictable. I marveled at the sights and even more at our Creator God, who made a world governed by laws, logic, and reason. Like the Psalmist David, I could say as he did, "When I look at your heavens, the work of your fingers, the moon, and the stars, which you have set in place, what is man that you are mindful of him, and the son of man that you care for him?" (Ps. 8:3-4).

My studies in medicine, though I had my feet firmly planted on the earth, similarly drew my eyes upward. In front of me on exam tables, in operating rooms, intensive care units, and outpatient offices were flesh and blood, fearfully and wonderfully designed physical human bodies. A heart that behaved in predictable ways, kidneys that filtered with precision, unlike any machine we have been able to create, and a nervous system that flashed with electricity, conveying signals at times faster than 200mph through the body. Here, too, not only in the complexity of the physical and the God who made it, our thoughts are drawn upward with the awareness that humans are not entirely physical. Something here is immaterial and unmeasured by physical instruments. This we call the soul or spirit. I marveled at our good Creator God, who saw fit to make us this way, as both a body and a soul, material and immaterial.

That humans are comprised of a physical body and immaterial spirit is evident. Cultures worldwide, without exception, support it; anthropology studies it; religion affirms it, and only naturalists deny it. They deny it based on no evidence but because of the inability of scientific inquiry to prove it.[5] Even atheists can support a spiritual nature, though they do not know from where it comes and may believe it to be snuffed out in death or else combined with other immaterial substances cosmically and indiscriminately.

Christians see our dual nature as our fragile, yet no less beautiful beginning, "Then the LORD God formed the man of the dust from the ground..." (Gen. 2:7a). Temporal dust formed an animated, not made intrinsically eternal but temporally, corporally, to exist for eternity sustained by Him who was and is and will be forever—God. Then He "breathed into his nostrils the breath of life; and man became a living soul" (Gen. 2:7b KJV). Though debate ranges as to what *Imago Dei* means, very few would debate what entered mankind at this point was related to that profound truth.

The importance of this dual nature and how I understood their interactions through Integrated Christian Psychiatry became apparent as I entered practice, principally in how I viewed pathology and healing.

First, it helped me define pathology as both a physical and spiritual condition that exists as a result of the fall.[6] To fall at the extremes of explaining psychopathology is easy: it's either all physical or all spiritual. Adherents of these positions view the failure of medications in certain instances as proof that the issue is spiritual in nature. The lack of healing following fervent prayer or anointing is given as evidence that we are dealing with a purely physical phenomenon. Conversely, medication success or those things that science can explain are presented as proof of naturalistic philosophy.

There is difficulty in stating to patients and ourselves that, as both physical and spiritual beings, psychopathology is not so easily defined. Somewhere between the extremes exists a messy middle that we, as Integrated Christian providers, undertake to explore with our patients (See Figure 2). This has implications for the way we pursue healing. We will explore this in depth in later chapters.

```
                God's Goodness in Creation
                         ↑
                         |
Physical  ←——————————————■——————————————→  Nonphysical
                    The Messy Middle
                         |
                         ↓
                The Brokenness of Our World
```

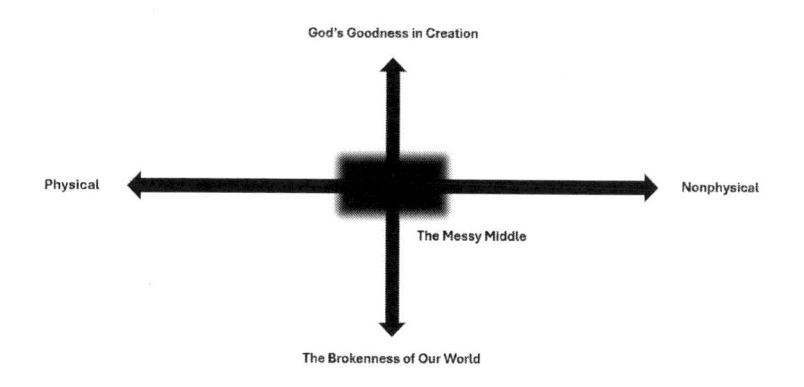

Figure 2. The place of psychiatry exists in the space of medicine (between the knowledge of the beauty of God's creation and the brokenness of our world) as well as in the interactions between the physical and non-physical. "The Messy Middle".

Second, it helped orient healing holistically, not neglecting any part of what it means to be made human. Because mental health conditions are not so easily separated into the physical and nonphysical, healing must be pursued holistically.

A case study may illustrate this relationship. Many have experienced the pain of insomnia. A night of poor sleep becomes two; it seems weeks have passed without a good night's rest. Patients toss and turn anxiously as the minutes pass, their bodies releasing fight-or-flight chemicals that propel them further from sleep. As a coping mechanism, they reach for their phones or turn on the television. The blue light coming from those screens indicates to the pineal gland in the brain that melatonin (a chemical released in preparation for sleep) is no longer needed; in a very real way, a digital sunrise has occurred. While the body reacts this way, the mind swirls with anxious thoughts about the future, regrets about the past, unfinished household chores, undecided plans, interpersonal conflicts, and financial troubles. This process is called rumination, the word taken from the animals who chew, swallow, and regurgitate their food to chew again several times; vivid and disturbing imagery that accurately portrays this mental process. Seeking relief, the Bible is opened to the words of Psalm 4, "In peace, I will both lie down and sleep; for you alone, O LORD, make me dwell in safety." Once a comfort, now, they seem a cruel taunt. *You could sleep if you were one of His children; see, He promised it.* Prayers become desperate, and God seems distant and cold. Doubts about our relationship with God become louder and our desperation stronger; when will the promises of the Psalms be a comfort once more?

With this clinical picture in view, it becomes easy to see how a sleeping pill alone is insufficient for healing a human composed of a physical body and an immaterial soul. Similarly, it is not so easy to separate the source of the insomnia. Did it begin with the ruminating psychology, the spiritual doubts, a poor diet, lack of exercise, hormonal imbalance?—the list continues. Integration is not integrating Christ into science or medicine as if we sprinkled Him into an already complete treatment plan. That is no more integrated than oil and water shaken in a jar are integrated; give it time, and they settle out. Integrated Christian psychiatry integrates and stewards the good gifts of science and medicine into our embodied, all-encompassing, daily walk with Jesus.

Should we take medications to the exclusion of prayer? Certainly not. Does renewed reading of scripture, turning to worship, or asking for the elders to anoint and pray as instructed in the book of James mean that we shouldn't check the levels of thyroid hormone circulating in the blood? It's a humbling process as a patient to sit in a gown on the flimsy paper of an exam table. How much more to stand alongside a pastor, counselor, medical doctor, and psychologist with our lives exposed, asking how we might steward this body and soul well?

Third, the integrated approach helped me to anticipate and praise God for our eternal existence in this embodied state.

For everyone who has been born of woman since the dawn of time at the moment of death something profoundly unnatural occurs: the separation of our body from our spirit. Made to exist for eternity as both a physical body and an immaterial soul, death wrenches them from one another. Yet, this separation is only temporary, for as Jesus confirmed as He confronted the Sadducees who rejected the resurrection, "And as for the dead being raised, have you not read in the book of Moses, in the passage about the bush, how God spoke to him, saying, 'I am the God of Abraham, and the God of Isaac, and the God of Jacob'? He is not God of the dead, but of the living." (Mark 12:26-27a).

Making beings of pure spirit is something God has experience with, the angels are made this way. Similarly, to stand at the edge of the Grand Canyon or in the Blue Ridge Mountains shows us He is more than capable of making what is physical stunningly beautiful to glorify himself. Yet we are not this way. We are unlike the angels, clothed with flesh of atoms and molecules. We are not like a mountain, nor are we like a deer, though made of carbon, oxygen, and nitrogen, because we have been made in the image of God.

Our Good Creator has purposely made us this way; it is also the way he entered the world and will exist forever in the second person of the Trinity, God the Son.[7] We can, with great confidence, proclaim as Aquinas did, *anima mea non est ego* (my soul is not me) and this is to God's glory because something about being both physical and immaterial shows his power.[8]

The integrated view orients the clinician properly in their understanding of psychopathology. With great sympathy, we see broken bodies and minds, and beneath our white coats, we know there lies a similarly fallen human. Then, with gratitude, we turn to the beaker, test tube, and microscope, all of which reveal pieces of God's handiwork and design, and, with thanksgiving, accept these gifts of common grace. Healing is viewed not as independent of the work of our Savior but as his work displayed powerfully.[9] The danger comes when any of these gifts become our God.

The danger of good gifts becoming idols is a risk for every human, but particularly for those who do not know Christ. A vacuum exists at the center of a non-Christian's being, and it presents as a restless search for meaning and purpose in seemingly anything and everything *but* God. Understanding humans as a body and a soul allows the Christian provider to serve the non-Christian more fully. The Biblical example of the Good Samaritan shows us that our faith and love may be displayed in our caring for someone who is in need. In our stewardship of God's good gifts in their lives, we are not neglecting their soul but meeting them exactly where they are at. St. Augustine writes in his *Confessions*,

"When we love our neighbor by giving him help for his bodily needs, our souls bear fruit in works of mercy proper to their kind, for they have seed in them according to their species... this we do, not only when it can be done with the ease with which grass runs to seed, but also by giving help and protection with all our strength. Then we are like a great tree bearing fruit, for we do good to a neighbor, if he is the victim of wrong, by rescuing him from the clutches of his assailant and providing him with the firm support of true justice, just as a tree affords the protection of its shade."[10]

As you draw near to these patients, you may find you begin to hear and feel the pull of that heart vacuum. As a provider, it may start to tug at the medication you prescribe, the therapies you employ, or your very self as a healer. Perhaps you feel that pull within yourself. In these moments, we do not rip away the medication, the therapy, or ourselves; we "preach the gospel at all times and if necessary use words."[11] We point them through action to our good God; if the door opens for us to share the gospel, we open the Word.

The secular world will criticize, saying we use medicine to proselytize. This is not the case. We do not exploit medicine for faith. We recognize that for ourselves as Christian providers, there isn't an act we can perform that is outside our walk with Christ. So we love as he loved and offer healing as he offered healing. Jesus healed many. Some sought him out; others, I'm sure, happened upon Him and gratefully accepted His healing.

We are very overt about our Christian faith at my practice, so I was surprised the first time an atheist sought my care (a more common occurrence than I initially thought). After meeting for quite some time, I asked him, "Can I ask why you chose to come here to this practice?" he sat back and thought, "Initially, you were the only one accepting patients, but now it's because I feel like I can talk to you and that you truly care for me."

Confidently I can say he felt that way because I did care for him. I see him as a physical body and mind in need of healing and an immaterial soul and image bearer of God. That's more than worthy of my attention and love and I will do everything within my power to employ medical knowledge that he might be made well.

For Christians, we are sensitive to the dangers of idolatry in any good gift, so we walk with them carefully, employing good gifts with sensitivity to their source of hope, which must always be fixed on Christ. Nevertheless, we accept them with thanksgiving.

In Christian circles, psychiatry can be controversial. Many worry that in healing suffering, we eliminate a potential way for someone to be drawn to Christ. I do not believe I (or any medication) is more powerful than the Holy Spirit. Are we, as Christians, so concerned about relieving hardship that might lead to faith because we put more faith in suffering to bring others to Christ than we do the Holy Spirit? We must remember: pain is not the reason people come to the lord; the Spirit is. He works in their hearts by the hearing of the word of God (Rom. 10:17). All who are called will come to Him.

The risk of good gifts becoming idols isn't the only reason psychiatry remains controversial in Christian circles. Perhaps another reason psychology can become so dangerous is because it occupies a space we do not understand clearly: that of the mind.

What We Call the Mind

In the fall of 2022, a computer artificial intelligence (AI) chatbot named ChatGPT was created and released. It took just five days for the system to gain over a million users, and for good reason. The computer language model can respond in near indistinguishable ways from humans. Conversations flow naturally, building on what has already been said, creating something different than a question and answer format, which was popular in the early age of the internet; this means talking to AI feels much differently. It learns as it speaks to you, correcting errors and gaining new information, which it then incorporates into its knowledge base for future conversations. On the surface it may seem that this machine has a mind, and when it discusses emotions, philosophy, art, or religion, that it may have a soul. This, of course, is absurd.

They cannot "think" as we do and do not have a mind or soul. They lack important elements of what it means to be made in the image of God. They do not have consciousness, an awareness of internal and external existence. They do not have sentience, the ability to experience feelings and sensations. They do not have a conscience or an innate sense of right and wrong. Something like each of these qualities can be programmed to *seem* like a conscience, sentience, or consciousness, but they are not intrinsic to the machine, and at best, they are caricatures of what we experience as humans.[12]

The mind is inseparably related to the brain, but the mind is not the brain. Paul, in confronting the Corinthian church regarding the use of tongues, wanted to differentiate words uttered in the spirit from words uttered with the mind while showing their interconnected nature, "What am I to do? I will pray with my spirit, but I will pray with my mind also; I will sing praise with my spirit, but I will sing with my mind also" (1 Cor. 14:15). Here, in the mind, we see our dual nature most clearly. The physical and nonphysical are distinct and yet unified in a state of true mental wellness.

We see this in pathology, damaged brains produce aberrations in the mind. We know many animals have brains, but they do not think as we do. There is clearly something physical and something nonphysical here. My anatomy professor used to say that our brain was a mass of fat and protein floating in a jar of dirty water and electricity. This pejorative statement conveys, in part, our frustrations as scientists in not understanding how that mass of flesh turns into this experience, consciousness, conscience, and sentience. It remains a mystery. But where physiology fails, metaphor and allegory prevail.

We may think of the mind as a plot of land, vast and ready for cultivation. Much of what grows there we have control over; we plant and harvest, replant, and re-harvest (this represents what we think). Other things we have less control over—who visits and spreads seed among what we plan to grow (those things spoken to us or about us). What we plant, we reap exponentially. A single seed yields much fruit; a single weed yields many others (the mind dramatically amplifies thoughts into action). Some have inherited land with more rocky soil, dryer climates, and heavier winds (those predispositions from genetic and epigenetic factors), yet even with the worst soil and the driest weather, we choose which seeds we plant. Tall trees tower over smaller shrubs, and frequently trodden locations make paths through the thicket. The longer and more frequently we walk the paths, the deeper the grooves become, and the harder it is to deviate to the right or left (our thought patterns and presets, the more they are thought, are reinforced and established as pattern and personality). This land has a purpose. Its intended use is to grow good fruit and glorify God with it (our thought life matters to God and can serve to glorify Him or be oriented in opposition to Him). This is why what we plant and what we harvest matters.

Jonathan Edwards said, "The will is the mind choosing." Influencing what we call the mind are desires and predilections, emotions, and others, which find their root in the Spirit. In the realm of faith, fallen minds incline toward sinful thoughts, and renewed minds more and more think of the things that are above. So, our task is to take the resource of the mind and steward it well to the glory of God. What we think about physically changes the structures and functions of the brain. Research into neuroplasticity has shown this.

Yet, as we work to steward our mind through meditating on God's word, correcting cognitive distortions and other faulty ways of thinking, we recognize the source of this renewal, "Who has put wisdom in the inward parts or given understanding to the mind?" (Job 38:36). It is God who grants wisdom and gives understanding. And, it is through the renewing of our mind that we are continued in the sanctification process and progressively better able to discern God's good and perfect will (Rom. 12:2). It is that same will with which we begin to desire; a renewed desire God is more than willing to grant (Ps. 37:4). There is much to be said about the mind, but for now suffice to say it is the principle subject of those who study psychology.[13] We sow into it. It is the primary way God has chosen to relate to us, and He is the source of its renewal from a fallen and sinful nature to a redeemed and God-glorifying nature that better perceives his will for our lives. That's no small thing.

Secular Psychology and Medicine

If you ask a clinician or psychologist, "What is psychology?" you will get answers that are different from those of the general public. This is a problem because the success of the field depends on the right understanding of its methods and theories. If they have never seen a mental health provider, most of the general public may have gathered all their knowledge about the field from bookstore shelves and television. To the detriment of the field, their understanding of mental wellness is relegated to what we call pop psychology.

Picking our books from the best-seller list of a psychology section may give the impression that happiness and worldly success are the goals of this field.

However, if happiness is the goal of psychology, we are not doing well. A study conducted by the American Psychiatric Association on anxiety showed that 70% of Americans were anxious about their safety, 68% about their health, and 65% about their bills or expenses.[14] In terms of depression and suicide, we aren't faring much better. The *Psychiatric Times* reported in July of 2023 that after the inception of the new crisis line (988) just under a year prior, there had been 2.1 million contacts, including 1.43 million calls, 416,000 chats, and 281,000 texts.[15] While 988 has increased access to care, and we are optimistic, historical trends of suicide have steadily increased over time. The Centers for Disease Control reported that the suicide rate had increased by 35.2% from 2000-2018, and 2021 saw the largest jump during the 2001 to 2021 period to 14.1 deaths per 100,000 standard population.[16]

In reality, the goals of psychology are to describe, explain, predict, and change or control behavior and cognition. For some in the mental health field, happiness may be the goal they set for their patients, but it could be many other things. In my case, as outlined above, it is the good stewardship of the gifts of common grace in medicine and psychology to the ultimate end of glorifying God. It is not exclusively the end goal of a mental health practice but rather the means of describing, explaining, predicting, and changing that make it "psychology." This is why, although there are no chemical tests or analyses, psychology finds itself in the realm of science, the pursuit of which has similar aims.

The Christian attempting to educate themselves on psychology may encounter titles such as: *How to Be the Love You Seek: Break Cycles, Find Peace and Heal Your Relationships*, the description online states, "It is our heart's innate capacity to love that is the true source of all healing. When we tap into that power, we can become the love we seek." Or *Radical Acceptance: Embracing Your Life With the Heart of a Buddha*, in which the author writes, "Believing that something is wrong with us is a deep and tenacious suffering." Or *Unf*ck Your Brain: Getting Over Anxiety, Depression, Anger, Freak-Outs, and Triggers with Science* which uses shock value and humor to try to explain some of the advancements of science in assisting mental health.[17]

For Christians, it is necessary to wade through a mess of false information and misleading concepts to get to the core of psychology. Many take the easy but regretful approach of "throwing the baby out with the bathwater," but there are good gifts in psychology. It may be helpful to explore some of the major fields of psychological research and practice: psychodynamic, behavioral, humanistic, and biological psychology.

Psychodynamic Psychology. You cannot discuss psychology at length without mentioning Sigmund Freud. Freud's view of human psychology involved recognizing unconscious processes, repression and resistance, and a focus on human sexuality as drivers of behavior and cognition.

Though many remember psychoanalysis and Freud only for dimly lit rooms, Chaise lounges, and extensive talk of misaligned sexual desires, the truth is that modern psychology would not exist without the work of Sigmund Freud.

Freud's concepts of the Id, Ego, and Superego are one way of defining the internal war that occurs within each person, fighting against the pursuit of pure pleasure and restraining oneself to be a functioning member of society.

It is perhaps Freud who better understood the fallen, pleasure-seeking, immoral (though he wouldn't have used that word) flesh that exists in the heart of man.

Behavioral Psychology. The first two years of my psychology studies were spent studying Behavioral Science at Western Michigan University. Here, students watched rats in cages press levers and perform a variety of activities to produce a food reward.

The field of behavioral psychology was largely influenced by the work of B.F. Skinner and Pavlov who pioneered operant and classical conditioning, respectively.

Pavlov's work began by observing how dogs salivated at the sight of food, an unconscious association between food and the body's physiologic mechanisms. He wondered if he could cause dogs to salivate to a non-food stimulus on command, such as a bell, which he famously proved in the 1890s.

Years later, B.F. Skinner would explore how human behavior was influenced by internal and external reinforcement and painful stimuli.

Skinner believed that through reward and punishment systems, he could shape a human into whatever he would like, famously saying, "Give me a child, and I will shape him into anything."

Behavioral psychology has had great success in helping extinguish destructive behaviors such as smoking, alcohol abuse, and pornography use. In the business world, it has helped create incentive programs to increase productivity and quality of life. It has helped parents to guide children with autism or intellectual disability to live in greater levels of peace and increased functionality.

Humanistic Psychology. In contrast to Freud's psychoanalytic view, which focused on unconscious drivers of human behavior, humanistic psychology emerged to describe conscious drives. Two of these drives I mentioned in the introduction to this book: Maslow's concept of self-actualization and transcendence. Humanistic psychology focuses on a human's desire to reach its full potential.

Carl Rogers, another prominent psychologist in this movement, describes the differences between the "real self" and the "ideal self": who we are and would like to be. When these two concepts are not aligned, one can experience a sense of dissonance. Who among us has not felt this tension in our Christian walk? Perhaps Paul described it best as he lamented the ongoing war between what he wanted to do and what he found himself doing in Romans 7.

Rogers also describes "Conditions of Worth" which are important to an understanding of humanistic psychology. Conditions of Worth include those standards, rules, or conditions that we feel we must meet to be worthy of love and acceptance. Another way we might describe this concept from a Christian perspective is an incorrect or incomplete view of God's love for us and the fear of man.

Biological Psychology. It may have been phrenology that first explored the relationship between physical and mental processes. Late in the 18th century, German physician Franz Joseph Gall proposed that measuring the curvature, bumps, and minor variations on the skull could lead to reliable predictions about mental traits. While his theories were completely disproved, the concept that certain brain regions are responsible for particular behavioral and mental processes was later developed and remains the cornerstone of physical anthropology. Notably, the work of French physician Paul Broca in 1865 showed that damage to a particular region (now termed Broca's region) led to predictable difficulties with the production of speech. Later, Wilhelm Wundt published Principles of Physiological Psychology in 1879, earning him the title "The Father of Experimental Psychology."

Since that time, the field of neurology and neuroscience has emerged to explore the brain and its functions. Alongside these fields, the study of behavioral neuroscience seeks to study and understand the link between brain regions, matter, and neurotransmitters to understand human behavior.

Dangers. There are dangers in each of these theories. Time does not permit discussing them all (nor have all the dangers been discovered), but some are immediately evident.

Freud used psychoanalysis to explain the belief in God as a reaction to our inability to control natural disasters. A being we could appeal to in an attempt to control what we could not control. Of religion, he states, "Religion is a system of wishful illusions together with a disavowal of reality, such as we find nowhere else but in a state of blissful hallucinatory confusion. Religion's eleventh commandment is 'Thou shalt not question.'"[18]

A strictly behavioral approach to mental health ignores the mind entirely, something the Bible pays specific attention to and calls us to renewal (Rom. 12:2). In fact, we are called to offer all our minds in love to God (Mark 12:28-31). What behavioral psychology offers us instead is a focus on the principles of reward and punishment that unconsciously (or consciously) influence our behavior for good and ill.

Humanistic psychology argues that to dispel conditions of worth, therapists should exhibit "unconditional positive regard" for their patients. This is rooted in the humanistic principle that humans are basically good at the core, a concept we will argue against in a later chapter. If we refuse to acknowledge a heart's sinfulness, we will consistently be surprised by its overflow of evil acts.

A purely biological approach to mental health threatens to separate what cannot be separated, that of being a material physical body as well as a soul. There is a danger in pursuing scientific naturalism, which states that the physical is all that exists. In addition, though advancements have been made in our understanding of neuroscience, the biological components of many psychiatric medications, as well as the genetic causes and predispositions for mental health maladies, remain largely unknown.

The danger in each of these theories of practice can also be present in their misapplication and disordered goals. This is also why my practice does not utilize any of them exclusively or apply them indiscriminately. Each has positive applications, and all, if separated from our knowledge and study of self as in God, fall short of the name psychology, which finds its roots in the Greek *psukhe*, which means soul as much as it has come to mean mind.

Holistic Treatment. Emerging research continues to show that mental health conditions like depression and anxiety are more than a single entity but instead may represent a diverse group of conditions with different causes but similar presenting symptoms. Many have quoted the poor response to Selective Serotonin Reuptake Inhibitors (SSRIs) as evidence that they don't work. In large-scale studies, it can be difficult to differentiate the medication from placebo, yet, for those of us in practice, we have seen plenty of patients helped by these medications. True, some do not respond as we hoped, but many find significant relief. What if this were because "depression" was not one clinical entity, but several, that we were attempting to treat the same? We would anticipate poor responses with large trials. Take pain, for example. There are different types of pain, some caused by inflammation due to damage to muscle or other tissues, nerve pain, and psychosomatic pain. If each patient who had pain was given acetaminophen, some would respond well, others not at all. Large-scale studies of acetaminophen for "pain" would show smaller effect sizes.

Our understanding of the complex syndrome we call "Major

Depressive Disorder" is expanding. Some benefit from SSRIs, others require Serotonin and Norepinephrine Reuptake Inhibitors (SNRIs). Others may need a tricyclic antidepressant (TCA) or a monoamine oxidase inhibitor (MAOI). We must also remember that there are no pills to cure the effect of living in a fallen world or in unregenerate opposition towards God. Could it be that many are seeking relief from an unreconciled spiritual state through medication? I would believe so. Some patients may find that their depression responds well to other, lesser-known types of treatment. I believe strongly that the future of psychiatry will include many more investigations into inflammation theory and gut microbiome. Some have found that correcting their diet to include much less processed food, simple carbohydrates, and sugars (all of which are highly pro-inflammatory) significantly improved their mental health.[19,20] Diet recommendations are about more than just what we remove from patients' diets but also what we include. The majority of Americans are deficient in magnesium and omega-3 fatty acids. Even if we try to eat fish regularly, it can be difficult to find nutritious, wild-caught fish that contains high enough levels of the components that are good for our body and brain.[21,22]

The brain is not immune to systemic inflammation occurring in the body. I have seen plenty of patients with chronic and difficult-to-treat gut issues that, when corrected, notice their anxiety or depression improving. We shouldn't be surprised that foods that are good for the microbiome, such as kimchi, kefir, sauerkraut, Greek yogurt, kombucha, and others have preliminary data suggesting their benefit for mental health.[23,24] As humbling as it will be, it would not surprise me to one day be prescribing fecal transplantation (a method of taking a donor's good gut microbiome and using it to colonize a patient's poor gut flora), clinical studies are already underway for this emerging therapy.[25]

God has made our bodies and brains to function together; things don't occur in isolation from one another. Holistic care must incorporate recommendations for diet, exercise, and sleep, as well as investigations into inflammation and gut microbiome, and one's faith if it is to treat the whole individual.

There are also plenty of vitamins and supplements that have been shown to improve mental health. Many other countries outside the United States have utilized natural products for mental health treatment for decades. The naturally derived nutraceutical Silexan was produced by a German Pharmaceutical company and successfully used in depression and anxiety.[26] Only recently has it been produced and marketed within the United States.

This section is not meant to prescribe to all a uniform therapy of magnesium, fish oil, and exercise—it displays that we must not uniformly prescribe anything; each person's presentation is too unique to have a one-size-fits-all approach in psychiatry.

Medication. My role as a medical provider wasn't a felt reality until a patient handed me her prescription bottle. There, along with the medication name and dosage, directions, and quantity, in the smallest lettering was inscribed: "Prescriber: AONeill." I wrote the script weeks ago, but it didn't feel as real as it did then. Although I had weighed the medication and non-medication options for this particular patient several times, this time, it felt different. It was as though I were opening the bottle and handing her a pill at that very moment, saying, "Take this; it's my belief this is going to help."

I don't want to lose the gravity of what it means to write a prescription. The position of my practice regarding medications was and remains: "We hold strongly that medication does not constitute a lack of faith in God's ability to bring miraculous healing but that it may be prayerfully considered when appropriate and accepted with thanks as a gift from God." At my practice, if a script is written and handed to a patient (or more commonly now sent electronically to the pharmacy), the provider believes it is for the patient's benefit and will ultimately glorify God through its use.

I have written elsewhere about some of the most common objections to taking psychiatric medications as a Christian.[27] I want to present how medications may help us in our Christian walk.

Heart work is hard and requires clarity of thought and emotions to be done effectively. At a Christian Counseling and Education Foundation Conference in the fall of 2023, Dr. Mike Emlet spoke of the difficulty of heart work while strong emotions raged, saying it was "Like trying to do a deep sea diving expedition while there are hurricane force winds at the surface of the sea." Seeing someone in the intensity of a panic attack, the debilitating state of depression, or a destructive period of mania, know that God's good and true Words in scripture often don't make it into the heart in the way we would like. They can be outright rejected or produce the unintended result of appearing trite. Not that God's word is insufficient or ineffective in any way, but rather that its application by a well-intentioned friend, family member, or provider may be ill-timed and, as such, bordering on or blatantly unbiblical.

One of the most common reasons for referral to my practice

from counseling is that good work has been done in the past, but now it seems a roadblock (of the kind discussed above in anxiety, depression, mania, or other mental health concerns) has prevented further progress. I view my work in medicine as an augmentation of the work being done in counseling, not a different or standalone work. Studies support this. Medication alone is nowhere near as effective as medications in conjunction with good counseling.[28]

Fight or flight rarely leads to well-reasoned and Biblical responses to difficult situations. We may be surprised to see what someone does in an anxious state. Some have made life-altering career decisions, friendships, and marriages have ended, and some have physically hurt others or said things that left deep emotional wounds. Usually, following these events, the person laments, "I'm so sorry; I wasn't in my right mind." Though we are still responsible for our decisions, even in extremes of fight or flight, we can see the impact of stress hormones like epinephrine, norepinephrine, and cortisol on decision-making. Medications, though not the only thing that should be pursued in these cases, can help people respond more rationally, focusing on the Biblical principles they have "stored up in their heart" (Ps. 119:11).

One patient expressed it to me this way: After months of working in therapy, she lamented that she knew cognitively the truths that applied to her situation, but they felt miles above her reach. When the right medication was prescribed, she felt the floor had been lifted beneath her, and the truths she once knew cognitively now felt as if they had found a home in her heart.

Many patients have come to me on the wrong medication regimens. How do I know? I ask one simple question: "Do you feel more or less yourself on these medications?" I am firmly convinced the right medication regimen helps patients feel more themselves. In some severe cases of psychotic illness or bipolar disorder, our medications still have much to be improved upon, and some of the side effects are unpleasant; they are used because of the high risk of harm to self or others. Even in these cases, when science has not advanced far enough to weed out the unpleasant side effects, I still believe patients should feel as though they were returning to some level of who they were, some degree closer to "themselves" than before. How many times have I heard, "We got our mom (dad, sister, brother, friend, pastor) back" after they started the right medications? I love hearing that. God has made each person uniquely gifted and equipped for service to His Kingdom; it is not my job to numb or sedate but to encourage and strengthen a patient's ability to do what they have been called to do.

Briefly, there are some things that medicine is not. Psychiatric medications are not "happy pills"; they do not possess the ability to create happiness intrinsically; instead, they till the soil that, with the right thinking, allows for happiness or a positive attitude to be cultivated. Medicine is not a fix for life circumstances or interpersonal conflict. I've had many dragged into my office by another, hoping that some medication would solve the difficulties in their home. This is an unfortunate place to begin therapy; unwilling participants rarely possess the insight to make meaningful changes with or without medicine. Finally, medicine is not evidence of a lack of faith.[29] Using medication is not a "throwing in the towel" as if one "tried God and it didn't work, so let's try medication." Medicine and our faith are not mutually exclusive. Years of practice have evidenced how medicine can help us grow in our faith. God is glorified in our right stewardship of medicine and our faithful obedience to suffering. We must rightly see our good God in the things he has made. Elizabeth Barrett Browning said, "Earth's crammed with heaven, and every common bush afire with God; but only he who sees, takes off his shoes; the rest sit round it and pluck blackberries."[30] May we always see our loving heavenly Father in the good gifts he has given us and respond with a similar reverence.

The Preparation of Mental Health Professionals

How do we make stewards of these good gifts? Arguments can be made to send practitioners to school, to pursue a certificate, to have walked through personal trials throughout a long life, to seminary, or elsewhere. My argument is that it greatly depends on which gifts we ask mental health professionals to be stewards. Each is trained to make available certain gifts with wisdom to the body of Christ.

By law, those who wish to practice medicine must undergo training in the science of pharmacology, biology, physics, and mathematics, among other areas. Then, should they wish to apply that knowledge in the mental health field, there must be formal or informal training in applying those medicines to psychological maladies. For the provider who wishes to practice overtly Christian medicine, evidence of a faithful walk with Jesus would seem appropriate. I know of one Christian psychiatrist who listed the qualifications of an elder found in 1 Timothy 3:2-7 in the employment contract. Though the role of mental health provider is not a formal position within the church, I believe there is great wisdom in requiring that those who approach fellow Christians in mental health trouble be above reproach, sober-minded, self-controlled, respectable, hospitable, not violent, gentle, not quarrelsome, not a lover of money, and well thought of by outsiders.

What about the DSM? Few books are more emphasized in the preparation of a psychologist, psychiatrist, or counselor than the *Diagnostic and Statistical Manual for Mental Disorders (DSM)*. Yet, few books have caused more controversy from within and without the profession. From its contentious beginnings and conflict with Freudian psychoanalysts who saw mental illness as a conflict between internal drives to the widely reported removal of Transgenderism and Homosexuality from its list of disorders by a vote of members, each edition has had some level of controversy. Yet, the monumental task it set out to accomplish, describing and defining psychological disorders, has been largely successful if evaluated through its adoption by mainstream medicine and psychology.

Mental health differs from physical health, a relationship we will explore in detail in later chapters. We cannot draw blood levels to find depression, we have no scan to detect schizophrenia definitively, and anxiety, though it impacts almost every system within the body, is more or less an invisible illness. This does not mean that psychological disorders lack biological or neurologic basis. Genetic predispositions, epigenetic factors, anatomical brain matter changes, and neurotransmitter alterations, among many other factors, have all been implicated in mental health disorders. The 21st-century psychologist is stuck in the middle of physical and nonphysical contributors and presented with only symptoms from patients. Thus, the *DSM* becomes a potential bridge between observable symptoms and groupings of disorders observed over decades of research.

How does the clinician view this tool? First, it may be helpful to view the *DSM* from its shortcomings and then turn to its strengths.

The *DSM* is inadequate in explaining the psychological experience of humans. To be fair, it doesn't claim to, but even in its attempt to place disorders in categories and boxes, it falls short of the lived experience of patients. Many patients have experienced the uncomfortable squeeze of being labeled with a *DSM* diagnosis that partially fits but not entirely. For this, the *DSM* includes "Other Specified" and "Unspecified" categories for those cases that don't quite fit. This, though, rarely comforts patients looking for a "grand unifying label" to explain their situation.

So, because the *DSM* struggles to adequately explain human psychology or illness, does this mean we should throw out the entire book? I don't believe so. Training in psychopathology allows a framework, not a flowchart, for understanding and diagnosing mental disorders. Training in the *DSM* is not training in a dogma but in a systems-based, current, data-driven, best guess at categorizing and synthesizing what we know of psychology.

Where it is helpful, it should be applied; where it is not, it should not restrict the clinician. Only a patient-centered approach at the practice level and a clinician-centered approach at the administrative level can adequately care for the needs of communities, cities, and churches. Patients should be offered the best evidence-based care, including all its pros and cons, risks, and benefits. The only way this can happen is if clinicians are empowered to utilize and disregard tools such as the *DSM*.

Treating obsessive-compulsive disorder (OCD) is an excellent example of the helpfulness of the *DSM*. OCD is particularly distinct in its presentation. Patients are greatly comforted by seeing their experiences succinctly put into words by the *DSM*. And now that the diagnosis is identified, the majority get to work addressing and treating it at its source.

So, do all mental health professionals need every element of the above training? This wouldn't be feasible or ideal. Each has a part to play in caring for patients' mental health. I have worked alongside talented Biblical Counselors who lament their lack of medical knowledge or training yet have an understanding of Biblical text that illuminates God's Word in practical ways for patients. Some physicians struggle with bedside manner but can grasp complex biochemical interactions and pharmacology.

There are health and life coaches who require no collegiate training for their certification but know supplements far greater than I could ever hope to, and social workers who spend most of their time conducting home visits but have seen things that would leave me speechless, much less with any advice to give.

What is most important in the training of Christian providers to participate in mental health is the use of one's gifts and abilities, training and equipping, to the glory of God in the lives of patients. This comes through the following: knowledge of God's Word, his special revelation to us, a hunger for wisdom and to know the right application of the good gifts God has given, a seeking after discernment to see and know what only God can see and know, and finally the training in righteousness. Robert Murray McCheyne once stated, "The greatest need of my people is my personal holiness." In this case, what is true of the minister is true of those providing counsel.

There is another training of importance that cannot be understated, though by nature cannot be systematized or sought out-- that is the training only trial can provide. Psalm 119:71 states, "It is good for me that I was afflicted, that I might learn your statutes." There is, in the lives of those most sage providers, eyes filled with the pain of past trials. There are personal mental health struggles, grief and loss of loved ones, sickness, and disease, among countless others. Yet, it was through those trials that God was found to be greater, more steadfast, and more lovely so that they may say with confidence only experience provides, "God is good, and His plans for you are good," even amid pain and suffering. Charles Spurgeon, who struggled with episodes of deep depression, wrote:

> "I am afraid that all the grace I have got of my comfortable and easy times and happy hours might almost lie on a penny. But the good I have received from my sorrows and pains and grief is altogether incalculable. Affliction is… the best book in the minister's library."[31]

I believe the transformational view of Christian psychology best captures this aspect of an effective mental health provider:

> "With God in heart and Scripture in hand, the sage or spiritual psychologist enters into the created world of things, particularly humanity, to understand the thing itself, especially as it relates to the human good and growth."[32]

This "world of things" is indeed painful and instructive, and it produces, by the grace of God, sage providers who pass this wisdom onward through their practice of counseling, psychology, and psychiatry. Paul encouraged believers in 1 Corinthians by praising God, "who comforts us in all our affliction, so that we may be able to comfort those who are in any affliction, with the comfort with which we ourselves are comforted by God."

Adam O'Neill

CHAPTER 2

...THAT THROUGH MENTAL WELLNESS...

"O unexpected stroke, worse than death! Must I thus leave thee, Paradise? Thus leave Thee, native soil!"

EVE, PARADISE LOST

"Those who dive in the seas of affliction bring up the rarest pearls."

CHARLES SPURGEON

"When I am in the cellars of affliction, I look for the Lord's choicest wines."

SAMUEL RUTHERFORD

What does it mean to be mentally unwell? How do we define mental wellness? It is obvious to anyone who looks closely at themselves and the world that things are not as they should be. The fall has dramatically altered our physical, mental, and spiritual state before God. This chapter explores the implications of the fall and the presence of suffering in the world. It works to define the goals of Christian Psychiatry as a part of the redemptive work God is about here and now.

The Fall of Humans and the Impact on Our Mental State

The sharp, sterile edge of the scalpel effortlessly cut through the skin. The patient was draped in blue sterile cloth and fully under anesthesia, laid with arm extended and exposed. The patient was female and had a confirmed cancerous mass in her left breast, and our job was to determine the extent of its spread. Imaging had suggested that a lymph node in her left arm was larger than it should be, an indication of potential malignancy. "Let the psychiatrist do some of it," the surgeon said. By this time, it was well known that I was not specializing in surgery and had chosen to pursue a career in psychiatry. This fact didn't excuse me from surgical rotation in school. Because of this, I became known in the operating rooms as "The Psychiatrist."

I took my gloved hand and firmly grasped the lymph node. Indeed, larger than normal, firm, and fixed in place, not good signs. Delicately separating fat, vessels, and tissue from around the area, the surgeon and I exposed and removed the likely cancerous node, placing it in a sample container to be sent to the lab for analysis. The diagnosis of breast cancer had already changed this woman's life; would she soon find that it had spread? If so, the mastectomy wouldn't be enough. Would she need chemotherapy, radiation, or more surgery? *Who sinned, this woman or her father, that she should have this?* The thought flashed through my mind and just as quickly disappeared. I took off my gown, gloves, face mask, and shield and tossed them into the trash. I felt a wave of guilt, yet from my reading of scripture, I knew the unconscious thought was the same as Jesus' disciples: sickness and disease happened because someone did something wrong, right? As humans, we have a strong desire to view sickness as Holy retribution or a balancing of the scales of the universe. Despite the prevalence of this thinking, this isn't the view the Bible takes. Jesus response to the disciples' inquiry about the man born blind was clear, "It was not that this man sinned, or his parents, but that the works of God may be displayed in him" (John 9:3). What a comfort that even our hardships serve as opportunities to display the work of God.

Another might assume my patient lacked faith or should have prayed more fervently for healing. But looking at the lives of other saints, such as Joseph or Job, who suffered not because of a lack of faith but *because* of their great faith, proves suffering isn't diagnostic of a lack of faith.

Our minds jump to this causal relationship because suffering is, as Phillip Yancy's book of the same title says, "the question that never goes away." Suffering requires an answer. We inherently feel the disordered nature of sin, death, rejection, and grief and know it shouldn't be this way, so we look for causes.

One of the most common questions I get in clinical practice is, *is my mental health a result of sin?* The most straightforward answer, I believe, is first to clarify what is meant by sin. What I believe people most often mean when they ask is, *is my mental health issue a direct result of sins I have committed?* which is different from *is my mental health issue a result of original sin?* There are several reasons why this question is important to us.

Most principally, we seek a causal relationship between our present suffering and personal error. If we affirm that suffering is a form of disorder and believe wholeheartedly that only good comes from God, someone or something is at fault for the disorder. Deep down, no matter how much we affirm a loving and merciful Heavenly Father, there is an abiding knowledge of his justice and right punishment of evil. When we sin, our guilt makes us anxiously look for the consequences. To us, a sudden car breakdown or broken water heater can appear linked to that lustful thought, greedy act, or lie. We believe the balances of the universe must be settled, and these must be how our Creator and Judge rectify the account. George Matheson, writing of Job's suffering, says,

> "Remember that if Job had been conscious of the special sin which his friends imputed to him, his suffering, so far from needing patience, might have been a positive solace. Remorse *craves* a penalty. Goerge MacDonald in one of his fictions has the incident of a boy who robbed an orchard, and then, struck with remorse, went to the chief gardener and said, 'I stole apples; beat me.' The picture is true to the deepest instincts of human nature. The remorseful conscience *wants* to be beaten. Tell it that the outward sufferings of life have been sent to it as an expiation of the past, and it will no longer need patience to bear them; it will receive them as a balm."[33]

The truth is, even *if,* and it's a big if, your suffering were the result of personal sin, the accounts would not be settled.

Speaking with my patients, I do my best to console them; the price for your sin was not a broken car or water heater; it wasn't an episode of depression or a panic attack; the price was nothing less than the death of the very Son of God. That's an indescribably high cost. Perhaps we think these other things could atone for our disobedience against God because we think too little of sin. The glory of the gospel is that the "balances of the universe" have been settled and that He, by "canceling the record of debt" and "nailing it to the cross," the debt has been paid in full (Col. 2:14).

In the front of my Bible, I wrote a Greek word I learned in my undergraduate training, τετέλεσται (tetelestai). These were the last words of Jesus on the cross recorded in John's gospel. It means, among other uses, "it is finished". It was also used economically when a debt was paid. The ledger was brought out, and across the place where the debt was written, *tetelestai* was put in its place, essentially "paid in full". For those who have trusted Jesus as their savior, on the divine ledger, this is what is written next to the sin debt. A right understanding of sin, of its requiring nothing less than your death, paid substitutionarily by Jesus the Son of God, is the first step in a right understanding of sickness and suffering, mental health disorders included.

Like Jesus' disciples, we are right to look for sin when we see suffering and sickness, but we need to look a bit deeper and farther back than yesterday's stumbling with temptation. We need to first look back to our ancestral parents and the consequences of those actions, and second, we need to look deeper because the root and heart orientation that led to their fall is present within each of us: the stain of original sin.

Genesis tells us that in the beginning, God created the heavens and the earth; He formed and filled everything and proclaimed it as good. He made mankind in his image and breathed spirit into them. Many have debated what it means to be made *imago Dei*; there are a few I find compelling.[34] We, like our Father, are creative, have dominion over the earth and animals in it, and are made for relationships. There are many more ways we are not like our Creator. We were not eternal, cannot create from nothing (*ex nihilo),* are not self-sufficient (we depend on something else for our existence), are not all-powerful (omnipotent), all-knowing (omniscient), or everywhere at all times (omnipresent).[35]

Here, the ground is set for our fall. Placed in paradise, under the loving care of our Creator, we forgot (and wanted to forget) that though made in God's image, we are not God. Adam and Eve's disobedience sent shockwaves through paradise, and the world was never the same. Their eyes were opened, and they hid in fear from God, their protector. Sin and death entered the world, our biology and psychology twisted, and our spiritual state severed.

The root of sin that led our ancestral parents to disobey, the pride of thinking we know better than He who created us, is the same that leads us to think and act (in word and deed) in disobedience to God and his law. It is common for secular psychology to point to the good in humans, yet we know and can feel that any good is the exception, not the rule, "the heart is deceitful above all things, and beyond cure; who can understand it" (Jer. 17:9, NIV). We see it in young children when they deliberately reach for what they are told to avoid, in students cheating on exams, in corporate executives led away in handcuffs for fraud, and in courtrooms where murders, rape, and robbery are tried; we see it externally because it exists internally; at the heart, "For out of the heart come evil thoughts, murder, adultery, sexual immorality, theft, false witness, slander" (Matt. 15:19).

We aren't just sick; we are dead. It was common for Puritan authors to add the phrase "there is no health in us" to their confessional prayers. For this and other reasons, the Puritans have been caricatured as downers whose outlook on life and human nature is pessimistic and dark. This view of our fallenness, however, is not without Biblical justification; Paul writes we were "dead in the trespasses and sins" (Eph. 2:1). Not sick with an immune system to fight it off, not mostly good with a speck of bad, not even mostly bad with a speck of good (Paul says even his good deeds were as filthy rags in Philippians 3:8-9). Before Christ, we didn't have the strength or goodness in us to accept him; in fact, we didn't even have the goodness in us to see him as good. Our hearts oppose him, not believe and trust in him, "The natural person does not accept the things of the Spirit of God, for they are folly to him, and he is not able to understand them because they are spiritually discerned" (1 Cor. 2:14).

Through the Holy Spirit, through which no one can say Jesus is Lord (1 Cor. 12:3), we have been brought from death into life, from sin into salvation, and from sickness into health. Praise God for his mercy and grace to us! How does this reconciled, regenerated state coexist with our continued sin and suffering? The answer is found in a concept frequently called the "already and not yet."

Paul may seem a bit contradictory in describing his present state as a redeemed sinner saved by grace. He describes his conversion to faith and being set free (Rom. 8) and laments his continued sin, doing what he desired not to do (Rom. 7). He describes Christians as blessed with every spiritual blessing and seated with Christ in heavenly places (Eph. 1:3) and yet calls himself a wretched man longing to be free from this "body of death" (Rom. 7:24). Paul is not confused and these two truths can coexist simultaneously because of the "already and not yet" of our gospel. Jesus has come, purchasing for his chosen people life and freedom, yet we remain in a struggle against temptation and sin. He proclaims the Kingdom as having come, past tense, and as coming, future tense.

Jesus' ministry on earth *was* the inauguration of the Kingdom, and he showed this by ordering disorder wherever he went; in fact, this was the proof Jesus sent to be told to John the Baptist when he asked if Jesus was "the one who is to come," the Savior King replied to tell John, "the blind receive their sight and the lame walk, lepers are cleansed and the deaf hear, and the dead are raised up, and the poor have good news preached to them" (Matt. 11:5). Evidence of the revolution, the Kingdom come was not in political revolt as the Jewish people expected but in ordering brought to disorder wherever it was felt, and the disordered nature of the world was felt no more clearly than in the heart of man.

As his friends lowered the mat into the place where Jesus was teaching, I suppose they considered this an activity they only had to do once. Their friend was paralyzed, but this scheme to get him right at the feet of Jesus would solve the problem. Their friend, though lowered and paralyzed, would exit the house on his own two feet. With sweat on their brows and tired muscles, I'm sure they were shocked to hear what Jesus said, "Son, your sins are forgiven" (Mark 2:5). *Sins?* They knew their friend was paralyzed, but they didn't know Jesus was blind and couldn't see what healing he needed. Jesus knew the man's greatest need, and he provided healing in exactly the right area. The friends wouldn't be disappointed. Jesus demonstrates his love and power in the reordering of his physical health as well, and the man walks, taking his mat with him. Our savior does not neglect the body or heal only the soul, but he rightly understands our greatest need is reconciliation with the Father, and with him, whether now or in the future (this side of heaven or the other), physically, we will be healed. We have been healed "already," and we await our future healing "not yet."

So we have established that not all suffering is a result of personal sin or a lack of faith, that the fall and stain of original sin disordered our world and led to an impact on our biology, psychology, and spiritual state, that Jesus' life death and resurrection were both necessary and sufficient for our salvation and justification with God and that his ministry on earth was to bring order to the disorder, showing this by both miracles of physical healing and offering forgiveness, in effect, inaugurating the Kingdom here and now while we also await the fulfillment of his Kingdom in the future. The question remains: is suffering *ever* a result of sin? The answer, of course, is yes.

When I entered the room, the patient was hard at work on his laptop. I checked the chart to make sure I was in the right room, "end-stage alcoholic hepatitis, transplant denied, prognosis poor" was written as a summary of the last note. Noticing my presence, the patient sighed heavily and shut his computer screen, "Whatever you need to do, do it quickly; I don't have the time." I introduced myself as a student and asked how he was feeling; he responded, "It shouldn't be me in this bed; it should be one of those idiots out there." he gestured toward the window overlooking the streets of Philadelphia, "I have too much to offer the world." The patient went on to recount his work with an international corporation, his world travel, and his experiences with women, drugs, and, notably—alcohol. He showed me a project he was working on, which he explained would revolutionize how people lived and interacted with businesses, "I can't die, I have this and hundreds more ideas." I spoke with him only a few more times before scheduled rotations moved me from his service; each time, he rejected his condition, recounted his escapades, and disparaged every nurse who helped him over the course of his hospital stay.

A wise counselor once told me that we, in the mental health field, should be grace searchers, not sin searchers, meaning, as those who provide counsel we often look for sin when we should be looking for evidence of God's grace. I agree with this approach, but there are times when we don't have to dig for sin; it hits us in the face, and its natural consequences are obvious. Personal sin can lead to sickness. Abuse of alcohol and hepatitis, in the case of my patient, pride and the isolation to which it leads (I never once saw a visitor or call to my patient's room), among others. I'm not putting my patient on trial. As I described above, all of us stand guilty before God (Rom. 3:23), but what my patient provides is clear evidence that sin can lead to sickness in very direct ways. Selfishness so often leads to marital conflict, greed to dishonest gain, violence to injury and death. For those of us who are in Christ we have justification before God, but this doesn't mean we stop living in a world with natural consequences to our sin. By these consequences, we are reminded that God's commands are for our *good*, not pointless instructions by a scrupulous Creator.

There's another type of sickness we may encounter, but it's not punishment for sin; it's loving discipline from our Heavenly Father. I don't know if my patient was a Christian; he didn't profess faith, nor did his life display the fruit of a Christ-follower, but if he was, his sickness is not punishment; it is discipline. For the Christian, everything is purposed for our good, and God's glorification (Rom. 8:28), and we should not despise when God offers us correction through whatever means, sickness included (Heb. 12:5). It may seem we are splitting hairs. A comforting statement of what appeared to be "your sickness is not a result of sin" has moved to "but it's a result of original sin, certainly," and "it may be discipline from

God." When my patients ask if their sickness is a result of their sin, shouldn't I immediately respond, yes? I don't believe so. God's anger at their sin and vindication through their suffering is the precondition to their question. This is so far from the heart of God toward us that to say yes threatens to affirm a theology of works-based righteousness and personal atonement for wrongdoing. Our God stretches his arms out on the cross so that he may eternally stretch them forward to embrace you, his redeemed child, in love.

So, how do we respond as Christians walking through physical or mental hardship? First, we learn to see those outstretched arms and grasp them tightly. There is value in searching our hearts for sin, not out of fear of God's retribution, but out of loving obedience toward him. We also pursue health in whatever form God may bring it, whether through prayer or the careful attention of a physician. This search is something we do during office visits at my practice. We explore our faith, assess the body, take captive our thoughts, correct maladaptive coping skills and behaviors, and see God as good through it all. The comfort of this chapter is not in saying that your suffering is in no way a result of personal sin but in pointing to our Savior who has covered all our sin debt in full, sits alongside (and within us) in suffering, and provides good gifts in medicine, therapy, and many other common graces as we walk through life in this fallen world.

Another patient was middle-aged, his hair unkempt, his body and clothes covered in dirt. It was said he lived outside, often sleeping in the cemetery where he knew he would be alone. When others came to help him, they found him with bloody wounds from self-harm. They attempted to restrain him, but it seemed not even restraints on the arms and legs could subdue him any longer. The sound of his wailing struck fear into those who lived near him, kept them awake at night, and frightened their children. Help was limited; it was early in the first century AD.[36] It seemed he would suffer forever or else succumb to one of his wounds by infection or blood loss. That is until the Great Physician docked his boat on the shores of his town. What our Lord saw was a man broken and infected by the world. The stain of original sin and the death that follows him are as evident as they are in the tombs he lived among. He had compassion on him and healed him. When we see him next, he isn't bound; he is clothed and "in his right mind," and he desires to go with Jesus. We aren't told much about this patient's past; we don't know if he had any family, what sins he struggled with, or if he held a profession before he was incapacitated. We do know that he began to tell others "how much Jesus had done for him," and it was enough that "everyone marveled" (Mark 5:20).

Before we encounter the same Great Physician, we find ourselves among the tombs; in fact, we were born here. It's all we know. We, too, cry out and cut at our skin with rocks with anguish. Perhaps we numb the pain with vices, pass the pain along by abusing others, or fake a smile and stand up tall and pretend as if we aren't covered in mud and excrement. Then, in this state, Jesus has mercy on us and heals us so that we, like the man in Mark 5, can tell how much He has done for us.

As we walk this thorny, uncomfortable road, we will, from time to time, find ourselves beset with mental hardship. This time, we look to the cross and read *tetelestai* on our cosmic ledger and proclaim God's goodness not despite our illness but because of it. That He would look down and see us fit to take up this particular cross at this particular time, we can sing as the hymn proclaims, "O Joy, that seekest me through pain, I cannot close my heart to Thee; I trace the rainbow through the rain, and feel the promise is not vain, that morn shall tearless be."[37] This is the promise, that what was broken will be restored, what is fallen will be set right, and that "[Our] warfare is ended, that [our] iniquity is pardoned, that [we] have received from the LORD's hand double for all [our] sins" (Isa. 40:2).

The Goal of Christian Psychiatry

Whether it was the ancients crushing herbs to apply to a wound, smoke from a burning bundle of sage, blood-letting from a purposeful cut, or, more recently, milligrams of medication administered through an IV, the goal of medicine has been the same: diagnose, prevent, and cure disease. The medical model hinges on isolating a problem and the systematic application of interventions to treat that problem. We are very good at answering what, how, and why questions. What disease is ailing my patient? How is it impacting the body? Why is it occurring here and in this way? Medicine is descriptive in how it defines disease and prescriptive in offering interventions to treat it. There is, however, a question not included in this descriptive and prescriptive process with implications both inside and outside the clinic or hospital room. Its absence is felt but rarely discussed. More important than what, why, and how is *to what end* or *for what purpose?* When an animal is hurt, it may be able to identify the source that caused the pain, through instinct, develop a course of action best leading to healing, and take steps to avoid the same pain in the future, yet one thing we as humans can do that other animals cannot is ask for a purpose behind our pain.

There is a reason a depressed patient presents to psychiatry. A disorder marked by lack of motivation (amotivation), decreased interest in doing things (anhedonia), and even the decreased ability to feel emotions (asthenia) does not naturally tend towards action. Initiating with psychiatry is an unfortunately difficult and lengthy process. One of the first questions I often ask my patients, especially those who have suffered for years, is, *why now?* The patient who has struggled to get out of bed for months finds themselves dressed (to varying degrees), driven, parked, checked in, completed intake forms, and now stands ready to answer complex and difficult questions from a psychiatry provider. We should ask why. I have heard many answers: relational (my wife made me), vocational (I was going to lose my job), emotional (I missed my daughter's graduation), and the always illusive "I'm not sure, it just seemed like the right time." Whatever the reason, curing disease or disorder is not simply an academic "what" or "how" but the very applied "for what purpose."

Friedrich Nietzsche aptly writes, "He who has a why to live can bear almost any how." Viktor Frankl would utilize this concept in crafting logotherapy, his distinct therapy style aimed at finding meaning within suffering. His training as a psychiatrist provided him a perspective others didn't have as he was interred in a concentration camp during World War 2, led to the conclusion that the drive to press on amid pain was tied not to the severity of the suffering but to the extent or degree to which patients could find a sense of meaning or purpose to bear up under it. He tells of the increase in sudden overnight deaths around New Year as those who had bargained with themselves to endure the Nazi camp horrors with the hope of being liberated by the New Year passed away from exhaustion, malnutrition, starvation weeks, days, sometimes even minutes past the midnight hour on December 31st.[38]

Where we fix our eyes, the purpose, meaning, and goals we set for ourselves are not trivial or tertiary; they impact the success of our treatments (both pharmacologic and non-pharmacologic) and the impact of psychotherapy. While we all have goals for ourselves, especially regarding seeking treatment, part of my responsibility as a clinician is to align patients' personal goals with those most predictive of health.

Most patients are surprised when I tell them that my goal for them may differ from the goals they have for themselves. My goal as a clinician is to isolate and understand disease and to provide appropriate treatment. My goal as a Christian was given to me as a mandate by my savior, "Go therefore and make disciples of all nations, baptizing them in the name of the Father and of the Son and the Holy Spirit, teaching them to observe all that I have commanded you." (Matt. 28:19-20a). This dual role of clinician and Christian influences the direction of therapy and my goals for patients. My goal for Christian patients, most generally stated, is that they progress in their discipleship in the midst of their mental health trial. With this heart orientation of "picking up one's cross" and following in the footsteps of their Savior (who also suffered on this earth, called in Isaiah a man of sorrows acquainted with grief in Isa. 53:3), we have here a "why" that far surpasses the needs of any "how."

This does not mean that I wish my patients to continue to suffer, only that mental wellness may be pursued while suffering continues, as it may this side of heaven for varying lengths of time. This concept can be quite freeing for patients; many assume they may only be well if the pain stops (a burden that only increases angst and pain). As we orient towards discipleship, our suffering becomes a tool and teacher.

Discipleship within the context of mental wellness has three aims, which we will explore in detail in the following chapters: first, that patients grow in their knowledge of God, second that they are more daily conformed into the likeness of his son, and third, that they become more effective for the kingdom of God, for, "The harvest is plentiful, but the workers are few" (Matt. 9:37).

The three aims are also found in the High Priestly Prayer prayed by Jesus over his disciples and all believers for all time. Jesus affirms his role as revealing the knowledge of God to the disciples, "For I have given them the words that you gave me, and they have received them and have come to know in truth that I came from you; and they have believed that you sent me" (John 17:8). It is through this knowledge that they have come to increasingly resemble Christ, "Yours they were, and you gave them to me, and they have kept your word" (v6b) and later "Sanctify them in the truth; your word is truth" (v17). Then Jesus prays these disciples, who increasingly look less like the world, not be removed from the world but to go out into it and increase in their work for the Kingdom, "I do not ask that you take them out of the world, but that you keep them from the evil one" (v15) and "As you sent me into the world, so I have sent them into the world" (v18).

These three aims are not separate from the treatment of disease as a medical provider. As they work to transform us, they do so from the inside out and are simultaneously influenced by the state of our physical body. Though we will address these in detail in the proceeding chapters, we may outline them here.

First, we are to grow in our knowledge of God.

In the first chapter of John Calvin's *Institutes,* he writes,

> "Our wisdom, in so far as it ought to be deemed true and solid Wisdom, consists almost entirely of two parts: the knowledge of God and of ourselves. But as these are connected together by many ties, it is not easy to determine which of the two precedes and gives birth to the other. For, in the first place, no man can survey himself without forthwith turning his thoughts towards the God in whom he lives and moves; because it is perfectly obvious, that the endowments which we possess cannot possibly be from ourselves; nay, that our very being is nothing else than subsistence in God alone."

As such, psychology is not an independent self-exploration but a pursuit of knowledge of self as *in* God. We also see ourselves as separate from God, fallen, and sinful. Calvin said, "It is certain that man never achieves a clear knowledge of himself unless he has first looked upon God's face, and then descends from contemplating him to scrutinize himself." Thus, an exploration of mental health disorders and physical maladies is a discovery of the ways we have been impacted by the fall, disordered down to the very cellular level. We have a sense that when things go wrong, whether a physical deformity, congenital defect, mental anguish, or even a virus or bacterial infection, it is not how things *should* be. Knowledge of God and his attributes are plain to see (Rom. 1), and eternity set in our hearts (Eccles. 3:11). This intrinsic knowledge of God and the way he designed the world to ultimately work is what causes such discomfort when we see death or decay at any level.

As medical providers, we also participate in the redeeming work God is about. First, in the healing of physical ailments that plague us. Nursing wounds, setting broken bones, and eradicating cancer are an attempt to return our bodies to varying degrees of that perfect, healthy, pre-fall state. Second, we participate in healing disordered thinking, which so often leads us to catastrophizing, assumptions about how others feel, projecting onto others, among many other cognitive distortions. To be clear, those who are not in Christ have reason to assume the worst; the situation is dire, and souls are at stake, but for those who are in Christ, we pursue transformation by the "renewing of our minds," fixing our thoughts on the promises of God for his people, principally the hope of justification through Christ and an eternity spent with him.

As discussed earlier, pain is a powerful teacher and often the instrument of our sanctification. Yet the healing ointment, pain-removing medication, and surgeon's scalpel may also be God's method of sanctifying us. Relief of suffering is an ability rooted in common grace, and we give great thanks to God for it. Ultimately, healing of body and mind is of great importance, but it is only a small part of God's ultimate work to conform us to the likeness of his son, which is true health; this is our second aim.

There is a knowledge that "puffs up" (1 Cor. 8:1), but there is also a knowledge of God's Word that leads to right living. The psalmist writes, "I have hidden Your word in my heart that I might not sin against you" (Ps. 119:11). As we increasingly look more like Jesus in our attitudes, thoughts, and actions, we treat each other differently. We view ourselves not as isolated (in a world that feels increasingly more connected yet more alone than ever) but as a body in relationship with one another with Christ as the head. We practice radical hospitality, provide for one another's needs, and forgive one another as Christ forgave us. We weren't meant to walk this life alone, especially not in mental hardship. The body, becoming more like Christ and acting more like Christ to one another, changes us. Because of this, we begin to look differently to the world in ways that cause them to take notice.

Third, through this process we become more effective tools for unique service to the Kingdom.

The great commission's zenith is in Jesus' promise to be with us always (Matt. 28:20), but for what purpose? There is a reason he instructs the disciples to wait for the coming of the Holy Spirit before beginning their ministry work (Luke 24:49). It is because there is work to be done and they need the help and instruction that the indwelling presence of the Holy Spirit provides. Training in righteousness culminates in the fulfillment of the great commission. This is why the study and knowledge of God and conformity into the likeness of his Son by necessity results in work for the Kingdom. We are not called to cloistered worship but evangelistic outreach. Following Pentecost, after the coming of the Spirit, as tongues of fire fell over the disciples, they were driven out to preach. Peter proclaims the gospel, and 3,000 were added to their number that day (Acts 2:14-41).

This is why, in discussions with patients, I explain that my main goal for them is not that they live happy or pain-free lives but that through the treatment of mental disorders, they may become more effective tools for service, using the unique gifting and equipping provided by the Holy Spirit who lives inside of them.

With questions of purpose and meaning at the heart of success in therapy and in resiliency through suffering, the consequences of disordered goals are apparent. Apart from the goal to glorify God, as the Westminster Confession of Faith lists as the chief end of man, all other goals do not have the stability or strength to see us through the worst of suffering this world has to offer. It should be noted that while these goals are not inherently wrong when they become the "chief end," they ultimately disappoint.[39]

So far, we have seen that the purpose of medicine broadly is to diagnose, treat, and prevent disease through descriptive and prescriptive processes. I have argued that this approach, while answering many questions such as what, how, and why, fails to answer questions of purpose. These questions of meaning and purpose are not solely detached philosophical conversation starters but are at the heart of successful treatments.

I then argued that the greatest answer to "for what purpose" exists in the glorification of God through an increasing knowledge of self (psychology) in relation to him (theology), that through this knowledge, we work to be conformed into His likeness, and that this by necessity leads to works of increasing effectiveness in service to the Kingdom of God.

Suffering, as such, is one of the most powerful tools in this process in the ways it teaches us about ourselves and our fallen nature, beckons us into closer relationship with God as we are made to look increasingly more like Him through the process of sanctification, and are equipped through this painful process for unique service.

Nothing less than the pursuit of Christ being magnified in us is sufficient for the suffering of this world. Everything else falls short. When this aim is our focus, we can, like Paul the apostle, look at our present suffering and pray, "It is my eager expectation and hope that I will not be at all ashamed, but that with full courage now as always Christ will be honored in my body, whether by life or by death" (Phil. 1:20). So we turn to this knowledge of God and exploration of these truths (though far from exhaustive) that lead to our mental wellness.

Adam O'Neill

CHAPTER 3

...PATIENTS WILL GROW IN THEIR KNOWLEDGE OF GOD...

"We cannot worship God if we don't know God"

JOHN STOTT

God's ways are higher than our ways, and his thoughts are higher than our thoughts (Isa. 55-89). Who has given counsel to him (Isa. 40:13)? Who has comprehended him (Rom. 11:34)? No book could contain the full knowledge of God. I suppose even the knowledge revealed in Scripture that might be applied to mental health practice would be as numerous as the different experiences of God's people as they approach it for Wisdom. As such, this chapter is in no way meant to exhaustively describe applicable knowledge that might be helpful to patients; rather, it describes some of the fundamental truths that impact my practice of psychiatry directly.

Imagine a couple sitting before me, their marriage in trouble as they contemplate divorce. Among the many problems they have, one is the husband's lack of affirmation for his wife. One day, he shocks us by opening the session, "I know I don't say these types of things enough, but I love you. I love that you are gentle and kind; you make our house a home by filling it with joy and laughter. I think you are beautiful. You are as beautiful today as you were six years ago. I look into your beautiful blue eyes and remember our first date on the boardwalk in New Jersey. Or when we vacationed for our honeymoon on the beaches of Turks and Caicos. I look back on our five years of marriage and look forward to our future together." The wife's expression was a mixture of unease and frustration. I lean back in my chair with a firm understanding of why. I know from prior sessions that this couple met eight years ago and had married two years later. They had celebrated six years of marriage together. While the husband was correct that his wife was indeed gentle and kind, her eyes were green, and the location of their first date was in Philadelphia, not in New Jersey, on the boardwalk. The aspects of love he tries to convey are lost in the muddied waters of statements he should have known to be false.

We show our love for one another in one way through our desire to learn, commit to memory, and recall important details about them. That love is strengthened by remembering the "little things," those that only a devoted lover would. This is no different in our relationship with God. This principle is encapsulated in the call and response of Psalm 27, "You have said, 'Seek my face.' My heart says to you, 'Your face, LORD, do I seek.'"(v8).

Our pursuit of the right understanding of God in Theology is not trivial, secondary, or a distraction. Our desire to sing praises to Him that reflect His true nature and attributes is an expression of our love, and it is supremely important to our psychology.[40] AW Tozer wrote, "The man who comes to a right belief about God is relieved of ten thousand temporal problems."

Reformed theology, as seen in the teachings of Luther, Calvin, Zwingli, Knox, and others, is often criticized for its seemingly scrupulous approach to doctrine, especially by the modern evangelical church in the West.[41] It is in part because of this focus on theology and orderly worship style that those attending Reformed churches are often termed "The frozen chosen." To be fair, there is a right and a wrong way to communicate theological truth, and we err when we force Reformed thinking on those not ready to receive it.[42] Where there is no room for debate is when it is inferred that these things are unimportant or trivial.[43,44]

I have heard quoted, "Doctrine divides, but ministry unites." This seems to me to be internally inconsistent. The logic I follow is this: doctrine divides truth from error, and ministry should be rooted in doctrine. Therefore ministry will divide. It is comparable to the process of clashing worldviews between a provider and patient in treatment discussed in the preface to this book. That clash is therapeutic and should be explored, not avoided.[45]

Ministry separated from doctrine is much like a boat without a motor or an engine without gas.[46] We can all board this vessel, but soon, we will turn to one another with puzzled looks and ask, "Why aren't we going anywhere?" To carry the analogy further, a ministry without doctrine works as a barely acceptable vessel on calm seas, but we know our world does not provide calm seas, not for Christians. We are going to need a much sturdier ship.

What we explore in this section is orthopraxy as well as orthodoxy. Right theology should lead us to right worship (or living).[47] The principles we explore directly impact the practice of psychology and lead to a resilient practice of the healing arts. Doctrine's impact on psychology comes when it serves as a stabilizing, orienting, and strengthening application to the sufferer. Doctrine isn't just the engine; it's the ballast, compass, nails, and glue that keeps us secure and from being tossed about by the stormy seas of life.

This chapter discusses the five *solas* of the Reformation, the core tenants of Calvinism, confessions and creeds, and the stabilizing truth of God's sovereignty and goodness in the midst of a world of suffering.

The 5 *Solas*

We begin where the Reformation did: Luther's rejection of the Catholic church's doctrines that argued faith and works (as described by the church's authority) were necessary for salvation. In response to this, the reformers' writings contained (though not necessarily all together) the concepts of *sola gratia* (grace alone), *sola fide* (faith alone), *solus Christus* (Christ alone), *sola scriptura* (Scripture alone), and *soli Deo gloria* (to the glory of God alone).

The importance of the five *solas* are in what they point to: grace, faith, Christ, scripture, God's glory as well as what they negate (i.e. everything else). Like a lighthouse in a storm, the stabilizing presence of the *solas* was meant to guide the Christian pilgrim to land and avoid the pitfalls of additives that so often creep into faith. Faith *and* works, Grace *and* merit, Christ *and* the church's blessing, Scripture *and* papal edict, God's glory, *and* the glory of the church.

The Reformation must have felt like liberation. The shackles of works-righteousness fell. Gone were the indulgences for souls in purgatory, and a hunger for the Word of God to be accessible to the people grew exponentially.

A modern Christian may take for granted the impact of the *solas*; we should not forget that many faithful reformers died so that we might know these truths. Nevertheless, the impact on Christian psychology remains clarity and humility.

As much as religion is the application of theological concepts to the lived experience, the *solas* provided enormous clarity. Our understanding of the source of our salvation (*sola gratia*), of our participation in it (*sola fide*), its means (*sola Christus*), its revelation (*sola scriptura*), and its end (*soli Deo gloria*) defined in simplest terms the essence of the Gospel. The gospel Paul preached was not "of lofty speech or wisdom" (1 Cor. 2:1) but clear.

The *solas* drive us to humility, for, in reading them, we see that it is only faith in which we participate and that faith we understand as not coming from within ourselves but also provided by God. Social standing, financial means, priestly favor or absolution, penance and other works based righteousness which all inherently or through human corruption tend toward pride fell. In this way, the gospel is truly for *all* people.[48]

Calvinism

My progression in Christian thought is, in some ways, documented through the last chapter of my first book.[49] In it, I end with a question that plagued me through undergraduate training, graduate school, and the time before my beginning practice: *Is a fallen and redeemed world better than a world that never fell?* The question hinges on the presence or absence of free will. My entire life, I had argued that evil was a necessary trade-off to maintain the greater good of free will. I regularly told myself God didn't want machines to worship Him. What began as a simple irritancy, much like a pebble in a shoe, became like the pain of a sliver as I studied scripture through college, until in graduate school, I could take the discomfort no more and surrendered to Biblical truth. I could, like Charles Spurgeon, proclaim, "I am not a Calvinist by choice, but because I cannot help it." I fell exhausted at the feet of a sovereign God who, "from all eternity, did, by the most wise and holy counsel of His own will, freely, and unchangeably ordain whatsoever comes to pass."[50]

I turned to Calvin and his students' writings to discover truths that fundamentally shaped my approach to patients and the practice of medicine. Calvinism, colloquially discussed using the acronym TULIP, provided a foundation for how I viewed the nature and state of mankind, God's irresistible and effectual calling, election, and perseverance of His saints.

Total Depravity. At the time of this writing, the United States has been plagued by several mass shootings, many of them appearing completely random and without warning. The trials of these cases are widely televised. Reading the news following one particular sentencing, commentators remarked on every detail of the guilty man's appearance, demeanor, supposed psychological state, family history, and early childhood, among many other details. Viewership increases during these trials (and during the subsequent docuseries that inevitably air) because we are fascinated to understand how and why something like this could happen. Every grin, tear, and facial twitch made by the defendant is a potential clue into the flawed psychology of this human anomaly. Here, though, is the impact of the pervasiveness of a grand lie: that this criminal's diseased heart is the exception, not the norm, for humans.

The reformed Calvinist principle of total depravity acknowledges that the dead heart of sin rests inside every human born under the curse of original sin. Though not everyone will commit a mass shooting, our hearts are capable and regularly display their capacity for great evil as it's preset, not the exception.

In the early 1970s, Dr. Philip Zimbardo shocked the psychology community, and later, as it gained popularity—the world, with his experiment performed at Stanford University. In his makeshift prison, which was constructed in the basement of the psychology building, randomly assigned volunteers assumed the role of "prisoner" or "guard." Before long, the randomly assigned guards began abusing the prisoners in ways that horrified visiting researchers, which forced the experiment to end prematurely. Discussing the study, Zimbardo says, "I argue that we all have the capacity for love and evil--to be Mother Theresa, to be Hitler or Saddam Hussein. It's the situation that brings that out".[51] His first book on the study carries this same message, titled *The Lucifer Effect: Understanding How Good People Turn Evil*.

What Zimbardo's research uncovered, though, is less proof of how *good* people turn evil but how readily *evil* springs forth from the heart of everyone, even those who believe they are predominantly good. A heart that is good does not produce bad fruit nor vice versa, "Does a spring pour forth from the same opening both fresh and saltwater?" (James 3:11). That a uniform, as shown in the experiment, could turn a random volunteer into a merciless prison guard is just as much proof of the true orientation of our hearts as it is of the power of the uniform to bring it out. Speaking centuries earlier, John Dalberg-Acton famously said, "Power tends to corrupt, and absolute power corrupts absolutely."

Despite the pervasiveness of evidence that humans are not *mostly good*, the thrust of modern psychology has focused on the exact opposite (as discussed earlier in Chapter 1).[52] The view we hold regarding where truth and goodness are found is important to the practice of psychology. The practitioner who holds that truth and goodness lies within the heart of the patient inherently will seek to direct patients inward, to search and dig from deep within themselves what they need to heal their mental state. The practitioner who realizes that goodness exists outside the patient will direct them toward this Truth, which is the only necessary and sufficient source to take what was purely dead and oriented toward evil and regenerate it anew.

Secular psychologists may argue that pointing a depressed person to a greater understanding of total depravity is counter-therapeutic. I find this not to be the case. First, depressed patients regularly experience greater awareness of guilt and sin in their lives; presenting them with a false truth of the "goodness within" usually causes a strong dissonance as the discomfort of believing this false truth is like shoving a square peg into a round hole. Inwardly, we know ourselves to be sinful and fallen. Secondly, we rob our patients of understanding their great worth, as evidenced by the sacrifice of Jesus for them on the cross. We may take, for example, the exhortation given to those who do not view their sin as gravely, who are by all secular standards "not depressed," as given in Thomas Kelly's hymn *Stricken, Smitten and Afflicted*, "Ye who think of sin but lightly nor suppose the evil great, here may view its nature rightly, here its guilt may estimate. Mark the sacrifice appointed, see who bears the awful load; 'tis the Word, the Lord's Anointed, Son of Man and Son of God".[53] We cannot fully understand our true worth until we understand the price that was paid. A rightly oriented psychology acknowledges our total depravity.

Unconditional Election. Dale Carnegie, a writer and lecturer on interpersonal skills, famously said, "Remember that a person's name is to that person the sweetest and most important sound in any language."[54] We've experienced this. Walking into a social event where we feel we don't know anyone, only to hear our name exclaimed by someone from across the room. There's a clear sigh of relief. Someone *knows* us. That's what is communicated by our name; it isn't a declarative piece of information about us as much as it encompasses who we are. God knows you and has called you by name, "But now thus says the LORD, he who created you, O Jacob, he who formed you, O Israel: "Fear not, for I have redeemed you; *I have called you by name*, you are mine" (Isa. 43:1, emphasis mine).

There is, most profoundly, an enormous comfort in the thought that before the foundations of the world were laid, before the sea was told, "Thus far you shall come, and no farther, and here shall your proud waves be stayed," (Job 38:11) God knew you, and predestined you to be His, "even as he chose us in him before the foundation of the world, that we should be holy and blameless before him" (Eph. 1:4). What earthly trouble can sway you? What material loss could touch the riches of knowing the God of the universe foreknew you?

The God of the wind and waves, more powerful than hurricanes or tsunamis, is gentle enough to see your weak constitution and have mercy. The God who knows every thought before you think it desires and delights that you should pray to Him about what troubles you. The God who has treasure stored up in heaven greater than we could ever imagine is humble enough to empty himself to live and die among humans like you. The humility of knowing that it was not because of any good you would do or evil you would not that he chose you. Reformed theology is not religious scruples; it is the comfort of an almighty, all-knowing, all-powerful creator who knows you personally, the good and the bad, and yet has redeemed you specifically for his glory.

The criticism of this truth is that it produces pride in the heart of the called. This, however, results from an overemphasis on "election" and an underemphasis on "unconditional." In addition the doctrine of unconditional election without total depravity would produce pride in the heart. There was no good in us that would cause God to choose one over another. A right understanding of unconditional election should produce the utmost humility in the heart of a believer and is a balm for the psychologically troubled mind.

Limited Atonement. It seems that laundry detergents are getting exponentially better at cleaning. Walking through the cleaning isle, I've seen "50% more effective!", "double the strength of other leading brands!" "10x cleaning power," among others. I've been doing my own laundry for quite a while, and despite these advertisements, I'm not convinced my clothes are all that much cleaner than ten years ago. Effectiveness, however, is good for marketing because it gets at the heart of a buyer's purpose in purchasing. We want to know that something works, and perhaps though it works, it could work better than we know, so we always look for the next most effective product.

It may seem odd to mention laundry detergent when exploring the impact of limited atonement on psychology, but we have to understand our desire for things to work and work well before we understand the balm of limited atonement in believers' lives.

Jesus' death on the cross purchased, effectually and completely, the believer's salvation. Its application to the ledger of a sinner produces complete and total forgiveness every single time. There are none to whom this gift would be purchased for whom it would not be accomplished. That's the ultimate effectiveness. There are no subsequent versions of the gospel for us to find which are "10x more effective" or "double the strength."

The peace which this affords the Christian in their walk with God echoes forward from the *solas* discussed above. Grace alone, faith alone, in Christ alone has been provided fully and completely for those who are His and will be applied to their accounts without fail. The comfort of this application is sung in Wiliam Cowper's hymn, "Dear dying Lamb, thy precious blood, shall never lose its pow'r, *till all the ransomed Church of God, be saved*, to sin no more".[55] What powerful imagery— a redeemed Christian singing encouragement to the Lamb on the cross, replacing the jeering crowd, that His blood would never lose its power, that His bride the Church it would purchase fully and completely "till all the ransomed Church be saved to sin no more".

The doctrine of limited atonement should, in our minds and

hearts, unify the Body and encourage the evangelist.

Look around you next time you are in service. This is not the Iowa Caucus. These people did not find themselves here of their own choice or volition. They are here because they are chosen, and they are forgiven because the blood of Jesus has covered their sins. You and your brother and sister beside you were in the heart of God when he said, "Of those whom you gave me I have lost not one" (John 18:9).

The evangelist preaches the general call of the Spirit to all people from every tribe, tongue, and nation. That Christ died for "the world" does not mean He died for everyone in the world, but for those who are His scattered across the world's four corners. So when our evangelistic call lands on deaf ears, we do not grow discouraged, nor do we stop preaching; we preach all the more so that the general call of Christ's death may reach every ear, the specific call may reach effectually those who are His, as Dr. Ryan McGraw writes, "The Spirit opened Paul's mouth to preach Christ, but He opened Lydia's heart to receive Christ."[56]

Irresistible Grace. In the discussion on total depravity above I argued that the practitioner who recognizes that goodness and truth exist not within the patient inherently will direct a patient toward something outside themselves. The good news of this Truth is that its pull on the hearts of those He reaches is both necessary and sufficient to raise a dead soul.

The differences between Arminian and Calvinist thought in this area is through the analogy of a sick or dead person and the medicine needed to save them. Arminians would view the Holy Spirit as holding out the medication and the sick individual reaching up to take it to their mouths. Calvinists instead see the person as completely dead and requiring the Holy Spirit to apply this medication, reviving the heart and leading to the affirmation of the source of their regeneration as the God of Scripture.

For this truth, I view the most powerful scriptural evidence for the latter is the raising of Lazarus.

The last thing I remember was counting back from ten, yet here I sat in post-op recovery, a nurse recording my vitals and asking if I felt alright. I'd been through surgeries before, so I was familiar with this dazed, lost-time, experience. As I sat in the hospital bed, recovering from surgery to correct a congenital issue with one of my kidneys, I searched my memory to see if there was anything else I could remember about the past few hours. Clearly, a lot had happened; I was on a different bed, in another room, in a fresh gown, surrounded by new hospital staff. Slowly, pieces started coming back, "Ok, Adam, on three, we are going to move you, 1-2-3." I remember bracing slightly and feeling the cushion beneath me move. I reached up to feel something around my nose, "No, don't take that off," the nurse cautioned. I listened and removed my hand; *it's oxygen tubing,* I thought.

What surprised me most was that I was not a passive participant in this pre-surgical state. The nursing staff gave commands, and I listened and obeyed. I had some ability to assess and comply, and I'd hope that if they asked me to do something outlandish or immoral, I would have resisted, though any doctor would describe me as, to some degree, incapacitated by anesthesia.

As "dead to the world" as I might have felt, this is not what Lazarus experienced when Jesus called him out from his tomb.

He, unlike me, did not sit in post-op recovery, recalling his contribution to his newly resurrected self.

In him, we find the closest earthly example and archetype of our pre-conversion spiritual state. Dead beyond the possibility of recovery, this is evidenced by the presence of the statement, "[Jesus] found Lazarus had already been in the tomb for four days" (John 11:17). It is important that we ask what Lazarus contributed to his being raised from the dead. In fact, what did he contribute to being unbound by his cords? We may ask if Lazarus could resist the divine command from Jesus to come out (John 11:43).

What does this knowledge of irresistible grace mean for the life and psychology of a Christian?

We try so terribly hard all the time. We worry about our ability to accomplish things at work, at home, and at school. We fail, though we try again and again. We become anxious, frustrated, discouraged. When we think of our capacity to accomplish God's will in our lives, the weight falls on our shoulders as a crushing burden. To truly understand how the irresistible grace of God calms our anxious hearts, we must understand that this irresistible call is also an irresistible, assured perseverance, not because of you but because He who called you has staked his righteousness on accomplishing His divine will.

Perseverance of the Saints. If I had to choose a concern most commonly raised in Christian psychiatry, it would be assurance of salvation. For some, it is only a passing thought that causes a temporary unsettled feeling; for others, this "what if" becomes all-consuming. Some Christians feel compelled to pray and ask for forgiveness or salvation dozens of times daily.[57] My usual response is that they are not alone; in fact, they are surrounded by some of the greats of the faith. John Bunyan, Martin Luther, and St. John of the Cross, among others, are all suspected of having struggled with intrusive, often unrelenting concerns regarding their salvation.

The doctrine of the perseverance of the saints is meant for those who struggle. The gift of the Church from the Father to the Son is one He stewards well, "Of those whom you gave me I have lost not one" (John 18:9). It is Christ who holds the Saints in his hand and keeps them.

John Bunyan was released of his chains through this doctrine:

> "But one day, as I was passing in the field, and that too with some dashes on my conscience, fearing lest yet all was not right, suddenly this sentence fell upon my soul, Thy righteousness is in heaven; and methought withal, I saw, with the eyes of my soul, Jesus Christ at God's right hand; there, I say, as my righteousness; so that wherever I was, or whatever I was doing, my God could not say of me, He wants my righteousness, for that was just before him. I also saw, moreover, that it was not my good frame of heart that made my righteousness better, nor yet my bad frame that made my righteousness worse; for my righteousness was Jesus Christ himself, the same yesterday, to-day, and for ever."[58]

Just as the grace that saves does not come from within the heart of the unregenerate soul, so the sustaining grace descends, undeserved and unearned, by the sinner, and yet God provides, pursues, and sustains, "Now to him who is able to keep you from stumbling and to present you blameless before the presence of his glory with great joy…" (Jude 1:24).[59]

For the Christian struggling in their walk with God, thoughts of self-condemnation abound, *if only I tried harder*, *if I had more faith, there must be something I'm not doing*. Indeed, we should be searching our lives for things we might eliminate that do not reflect our new nature and begin practicing spiritual disciplines that lead us into greater conformity to Christ, but the most important thing we can do if we feel we lack grace is to *ask* for more.

When trials of life press in, we need God's grace. We need God's grace when we notice our weakness in body, mind, or soul. When we continually fail to do what we know we should do or do what we do not want to do, we need God's grace. Knowing the difference between what we are capable of, and what God commands of us led St. Augustine to proclaim, "Give what you command [O Lord], and then command whatever you will." This grace exists outside us and is granted and applied by God to us. This, I have discovered, is a truth that relieves the anxious mental state of one who believes it all rests on their shoulders. He must give what he commands, and He will keep us until the end.

Confessional Faith and Psychology

It may seem odd, or otherwise perfectly fitting, that the Book of Comfort, the Heidelberg Catechism, was penned in a time of conflict, often bloody, between the Lutherans and Calvinists on the issue of the Lord's Supper and the Person of Christ. The conflict that Prince Frederick III inherited as elector of the Palatinate region of Germany required wisdom, so daily, he asked it from God and prayed the words of Psalm 31. It became clear that a catechism would best unify a divided church, so he commissioned Zacharius Ursinus and Caspar Olevianus.

Against the backdrop of beautifully mountainous Heidelberg, Germany, in 1563, like a balm, the words of question one were spoken into the conflict: "What is your only comfort in life and death? That I am not my own, but belong with body and soul, both in life and in death, to my faithful savior Jesus Christ...". When a group of delegates from all across Europe came to vote on the catechism's text, there was not a single dissenter or edit, and they rejoiced by staying a little longer to celebrate the Lord's Supper together.

Some 80 years later, 400 miles from Heidelberg, Germany, a much larger group met with a similar purpose. The Westminster Assembly met to produce a document to unite the Church of England and the Church of Scotland.

Though it took five years and volumes of debate, the Westminster Standards were published. It was to these two giant but separate churches that the unifying direction of man stood as a signpost: "What is the chief end of man? Man's chief end is to glorify God and to enjoy him forever."[60]

The process of meeting together in this way is as old as the apostles. Unity among believers required gathering, discussing, and making decisions on contentious topics. It was to this Jerusalem Council in AD 50, reported in Acts 15 that Barnabas and Paul presented what had been seen among the Gentiles during their missionary journeys. After "there had been much debate," James proposes, "...we should not trouble those of the Gentiles who turn to God, but should write to them to abstain from the things polluted by idols, and from sexual immorality, and from what has been strangled, and from blood." So, the letter was drafted and sent in a circular to the churches.

The Christian faith is confessional, and this matters to the practice of psychology. I think it best to list the importance of confessional faith as a set of affirmations and denials.[61]

Confessional faith is an affirmation of the source of truth. Confessions, creeds, and catechisms do not have intrinsic authority but rather derive authority from scripture and rest in subjection to the infallible Word. We can proclaim with Peter that "His divine power has granted to us all things that pertain to life and godliness, through the knowledge of him who called us to his own glory and excellence..." (2 Pet. 1:3), which he revealed to us through His Word though written thousands of years ago remains relevant and assists us in navigating a world which searches for truth. Opening the Westminster Standards, we find the Biblical references, which, when displayed, outnumber the words of the Divines. There are, among the pages, no new truths or revelations outside scripture, only a statement of affirmation and assent to what has been given by God.

Confessional faith denies the modern-day concept of moral subjectivism, which permeates secular psychology and thought. In a world progressively moving toward moral relativism, that it could be stated with conviction that something is universally true is becoming more controversial. Major denominations have needed to produce updates to their statements of faith and confessions to clarify their position on the role of gender, the definition of marriage, and positions on abortion, among other issues. It is not uncommon in psychology to see practitioners pointing clients inward and to feelings to determine what is "true for them," which may not necessarily be true for someone else.[62] We neglect the stabilizing nature of knowing that truth is external and needs to be brought internally rather than vice versa.

Confessional faith is an affirmation of the process of catechizing our children, that the primary burden of teaching and training children is the family unit, which God has ordained, guided, and directed through the church. We see, progressively, that topics that parents used to be responsible for are now occurring in standardized education. Sex education, gender roles, understanding emotions and what to do with them, world religions and worldviews, ethics, and others are now delivered by teachers in school rather than around dinner tables by parents. The impact of underemphasizing the family and outsourcing education to the State can hardly be understated. Catechism affirms that conversation, not necessarily access to literature (i.e., handing someone a book), is one of the most important ways parents will convey truth to their children.

Confessional faith is a denial that age precludes someone from a slow drift from truth without foundations set in Biblical Standards. Though we catechize children, we all need to be reminded of truth through this process and through a regular reaffirmation of what we believe to be true. Our tendency is toward a slow drift away from truth without the stabilizing presence of confessional faith.

Confessional faith is a denial of "chronological snobbery."[63] Sitting with our laptops in coffee shops or on airplanes in the sky, we can be tempted to believe we have a greater understanding of Truth than those who came before. How could we not? Technology and knowledge have advanced exponentially. Time's passing alone, however, does not alter the truthfulness of Truth. Knowledge may grow, but it does not change truth; it may reveal that what was proclaimed to be true was false (such as the belief that the Sun revolves around the Earth), but truth has not changed; falsehood has been revealed to have masqueraded as truth for a period of time. Knowledge can also reveal a change in truth by degree (such as our understanding of the way to model atoms and molecules or subatomic particles), but what was said before was not false but an incomplete truth. Confessional faith is the bold affirmation that what has been said before is Truth in substance and degree and will not change. This is rare and should be treasured by modern Christians.

In a sermon titled *Constraining Love*, J. Gresham Machen highlighted the importance of a confessional faith, calling it a "privilege",

> "What a privilege to proclaim not some partial system of truth but the full, glorious system which God has revealed in His Word, and which is summarized in the wonderful Standards of our Faith! What a privilege to get those hallowed instruments, in which that truth is summarized, down from the shelf and write them in patient instruction, by the blessing of the Holy Spirit, upon the tablets of the children's hearts! What a privilege to present our historic Standards in all their fulness in the pulpit and at the teacher's desk and in the Christian home! What a privilege to do that for the one reason that those Standards present, not a 'man-made creed,' but what God has told us in His holy Word! What a privilege to proclaim that same system of divine truth to the unsaved! What a privilege to carry the message of the cross, unshackled by compromising associations, to all the world! What a privilege to send it to foreign lands! What a privilege to proclaim it to the souls of people who sit in nominally Christian churches and starve for lack of the bread of life! Oh, yes, what a privilege and what a joy, my brethren!"

Reformed Theology in Summary

The above discussion has attempted to point to Truths that have real applications to the practice of psychology and one's experience of walking with the Lord. It may be argued that there is some middle position that allows for flexibility in denominational beliefs, and indeed, there is. Still, I believe the implications of *these* particular truths are too great to allow for a middle position. The nature of salvation expressed in the *solas* of the Reformation separates us from those in the Catholic faith in as much of a dramatic fashion as they did during the Reformation in 1517 when Martin Luther nailed his

95 Theses to the church door in Wittenburg, Germany. We are Calvinists because we see ourselves as totally depraved but possessing an irresistible and unconditional grace that flows from the work of Christ on behalf of His people on the cross, which keeps us until the end. We affirm these truths through historic confessions and creeds and catechize our children in the truth of scripture.

To summarize, we are reformed because we are not Catholic; we are catholic because we are in Christ, and we are orthodox because we believe what He has revealed in His Word. We have best communicated this Word in the work of minds and through the mouths of earthly saints through the confessions and creeds of the historic church, which have condemned heresy and decried blasphemy through the ages, and we pass this teaching along to our children (though not exclusively), through catechism. This is the essence of orthodoxy (right teaching) and has drastic implications for orthopraxy (right living). The stability, comfort, and awesome power of this doctrine change mental health and align us with the teaching of Scripture.

God's Sovereignty in a World of Suffering

Knowledge of God's sovereignty over good and evil is one of the most comforting and frightening truths we wrestle with as Christians. There is an approach to exploring God's sovereignty theoretically, talking of lofty theological concepts like sovereign and permissive will, concurrence, and his sovereign choice via supra or infralapsarianism. Yet, I believe the best way to approach the truth of our sovereign God is through the stories of his people and the good and evil that befalls them on the road to sanctification. This is how our gospel approaches us, through narrative, and often communicates truth to our hearts better than any theology textbook could. The following sections tell stories of saints and an earthly, temporal guess at the good already produced in a world of suffering. If we see this good now, how radiant will be the good when all is made clear in the new heavens and earth?

George – Suffering that produced a heart of praise. Born in 1842, young George Matheson had all the makings of a promising academic career. He had published two books on theology and graduated with honors in classics, philosophy, and logic. He prepared for advanced study and a trajectory that would take him to be one of Scotland's most influential theological leaders. Then, at the age of 20, he began to lose his vision, suffering from a condition for which the doctors of his day had no cure. Society did not provide for those with disabilities (physical or mental); as such, blindness was a sentence of destitution. When he broke the news to his fiancé, she could not bear the prospect of living and caring for him for the remainder of her life and broke off their engagement. Matheson was devastated. Professionally and personally, his life lay in ruins.

He did, with the help of his sister, complete his degree and become a minister. Though his world was dark, his preaching brought light to thousands. Though his situation was far from perfect, he felt his life and work had purpose, and he was content.

His sister's companionship ended one day in 1882 when she prepared to get married and start a family of her own. Leaving to prepare for the ceremony, Matheson was left alone in the house, quiet and with darkness surrounding him, no doubt thinking both of his own failed engagement and the life that could have been. In this darkness and suffering, a heart of worship sprang from the depths. Here, he penned the words to one of his most famous hymns:

> Oh love that will not let me go / I rest my weary soul in thee / I give thee back the life I owe / That in thine ocean depths its flow / May richer, fuller be.

Speaking of his hymn, Matheson writes,

> "My hymn was composed in the manse of Innellan on the evening of the 6th of June, 1882. . . . Something happened to me, which was known only to myself, and which caused me the most severe mental suffering. The hymn was the fruit of that suffering. It was the quickest bit of work I ever did in my life. I had the impression rather of having it dictated to me by some inward voice than of working it out myself. I am quite sure that the whole work was completed in five minutes, and equally sure it never received at my hands any retouching or correction. I have no natural gift of rhythm. All the other verses I have ever written are manufactured articles; this came like a dayspring from on high. I have never been able to gain once more the same fervor in verse."

In 1885, Queen Victoria invited Matheson to preach. His sermon so moved her that she had it printed and published for others to read. He titled his sermon "The Patience of Job," no doubt moved by another man weary with suffering who found a life given back to God, "May richer, fuller be."[64]

Elisabeth Elliot describes it best in the retelling of Matheson's life in her book *The Path of Loneliness*,

> "Matheson turned his thoughts away from the woman he had lost, away from the powerful temptations to self-pity, resentment, bitterness toward God, skepticism of His Word, and selfish isolation which might so quickly have overcome him, and lifted up his 'weary soul' to a far greater Love-- one that would never let him go. In the words 'I give Thee back the life I

owe' Matheson understood that there was something he could do with his suffering. It was the great lesson of the Cross: surrender. If Jesus had been unwilling to surrender to humanity's worst crime, humanity's salvation would have been impossible... We live because He died. The power of the Cross is not exemption from suffering but the very transformation of suffering".[65]

George Matheson saw his suffering not as a cosmic accident but as the work of a sovereign God in his life.

Joni – Suffering that Produced a Life of Impact. Joni Eareckson Tada was a gifted young athlete. As frequently happens among those gifted with physical prowess, her athletic career became her life. After celebrating her high school graduation and recent superlative as "best athlete," she went to the Chesapeake Bay and attempted an inward pike dive off a raft. Her head and neck slammed against the moving sandbar beneath the water. Her arms and legs went limp. She was paralyzed from the neck down.

She scoured scripture for verses of healing, attended prayer meetings, confessed sin, was anointed with oil, and had elders pray over her, and yet she was not healed. As the months and years passed, it became clear her paralysis was permanent. The life she had planned to live was ripped from her hands, and a new life, one of dependency on others for daily tasks and restriction to a wheelchair, took its place.

Though not overnight, her purpose and mission for Christ took shape. The unique way she would glorify God, it seemed, had wheels, not legs. Her ministry "Joni and Friends" has included books, camps and retreats, a radio program, a television show, and countless other charitable programs that provide wheelchairs and assistance to those both nationally and overseas with disabilities.

Writing of her injury, she states,

> "A 'no' answer to my request for a miraculous physical healing has meant purged sin, a love for the lost, increased compassion, stretched hope, an appetite for grace, an increase of faith, a happy longing for heaven, a desire to serve, a delight in prayer, and a hunger for his Word. Oh, bless the stern schoolmaster that is my wheelchair!". [66]

Beyond all that she has done for others as a result of her injury, she sees the hand of her savior working purposeful sanctification in her life and preparing her for her eternal home where she will no longer be in a wheelchair. Speaking of this freedom, she says,

> "I hope that I can have my wheelchair in heaven with me…I would walk up to my savior and I would say, 'Lord Jesus you see that wheelchair there, before you send it to Hell I want to tell you something…the weaker I was in that thing the harder I leaned on you and the harder I leaned on you the stronger I discovered you to be. I'm so grateful.'"

God didn't watch Joni do that dive and gasp, He knew what she was doing and was sovereign in it, both over her and the sand bar He moved beneath the neck of a child he dearly loved.

Joseph – Suffering that Produced a Hope of Heaven. A young man sat in my office; we'll call him Joseph. The scars on his neck and chest told the story of repeated surgeries to correct a congenital issue the doctors had struggled to control. It wasn't for this concern that he had come to me, however. Joseph presented to me because he suffered from severe schizophrenia, which presented as dark hallucinations and taunting voices. Some were nonsensical, fleeting shadows or dark shapes. Others were clearer and darker, taking the form of a family member who had abused him. In the night, these figures would draw as close to his face as only a hallucination can to hiss and taunt him. To stop the images, he would hit himself in a desperate attempt to make it stop.

In my sessions, we chatted about his hallucinations, but we also talked about comic books. Joseph loved superheroes. To distract him from his hallucinations he would read or watch Marvel or DC movies. During one session, we discussed Batman; Joseph remarked that though he liked him, the movies could be rather dark—I agreed. I began to reflect on the dark hero of Gotham City. Suddenly, it dawned on me; I recalled that Joseph wanted to write a comic featuring a superhero one day, "Joseph," I asked, "if you write a story of a hero, where will their story begin?" He thought for a moment but was uncertain, so I prompted him, "Where did Batman begin?" He knew without hesitation and recounted Bruce Wayne's life as part of a wealthy socialite and philanthropist family, his traumatizing fear of bats, and the sudden loss of his parents. I could see him internally processing this tragic origin story. "What about Superman?" I asked, to which he quickly replied, "The loss of his home planet Krypton."[67] We began to assess other origin stories: Iron Man, Captain Marvel, Shazam, and the X-Men, among others. Each had experienced (and many continued to experience) the impact of a painful past but had chosen to persevere despite the hardship.

One day, after a particularly difficult week, Joseph asked me, "Will I have to fight these images in heaven?" Joseph knew Jesus; he trusted him for his salvation and believed that he had fought and won his redemption, but here, in the innocence of his question to me, was his unawareness of the beautiful fact that Jesus had fought and won his victory over every lingering hallucination, every painful memory of abuse, every sleepless night. This physical and mental healing is included in the prize he is handed at the end of his race. I remembered the superheroes we discussed and saw Joseph among them. Though he couldn't see it, Joseph carried a heavy cross, but it wasn't one he carried alone, and it wasn't one he would carry forever.

Joseph's influence in my life caused me to long for the hope of heaven and the physical and mental healing we will all experience there. His love of comics pointed me to another hero whose origin story begins in a manger and leads him to a cross but culminates in an empty tomb and a promised return to make all things new. God is sovereign in Joseph's life hardships as much as He is in the future healing He has planned for him.

John Doe – Suffering that Produces Choruses in Heaven. There's a story I'd like to tell you, but I can't. It's filled with deep pain and hardship and uncertain ways that the struggle leads to God's glory and their good. I'm unable to tell you this story because it's too personal or private or protected by medical privacy laws. The story that goes in this space is one I don't know; it's one no one living but the person experiencing it will know. Maybe this story is yours. Perhaps you are uncertain if anyone will ever truly know what you've experienced. Maybe it's difficult to proclaim a God who is sovereign over suffering, given what you are walking through. Maybe it seems like, after reading the stories above, that this suffering is so unbearable precisely because it feels like it has no purpose and produced no fruit.

In my office is a library that contains a mixture of books helpful for me throughout the day seeing patients: medical textbooks and references, poetry, philosophy, both secular and religious, and many books on faith and the Christian walk. Scanning each of these sections, you will find a theme, a common question asked by poets, philosophers, and physicians alike: "What is the purpose of suffering?" Those who proclaim a sovereign God must come to terms with suffering.[68]

So far, we have been introduced to a few people who suffered greatly but saw the sovereign work of God in their lives. He was glorified, and somehow, though they could only see it from the far side of their suffering, they received the most good. But what of those who suffer and no one sees? What of the sufferer who produces no books, foundations, or charities and doesn't go into ministry or missions? What is God's purpose behind their suffering? I do not have all the answers for those experiencing deep suffering, nor do I believe, as good as it may be, that a charity, trophy, or book could "make right" what has been wronged. I do know, however, that we never suffer without an audience.

If the apostle's earthly ministry was marked by one thing, it would be relentless persecution. To the Jewish leaders of their day, they represented a threat to their authority, which would unsettle political power and financial standing locally, and a force capable of destabilizing the already tenuous relationship they had with secular governors dispatched by Rome to survey and levy taxes on the region. The apostle Paul, in his travels to preach the gospel to the Gentiles, recounts in his letter to the Corinthians, his trials,

> "Five times I received at the hands of the Jews the forty lashes less one. Three times I was beaten with rods. Once I was stoned. Three times I was shipwrecked; a night and a day I was adrift at sea; on frequent journeys, in danger from rivers, danger from robbers, danger from my own people, danger from Gentiles, danger in the city, danger in the wilderness, danger at sea, danger from false brothers; in toil and hardship, through many a sleepless night, in hunger and thirst, often without food, in cold and exposure. And, apart from other things, there is the daily pressure on me of my anxiety for all the churches" (2 Cor. 11:24-28).

In each of these experiences, any one of which was likely to lead to his death, he knows they recall his words from his first letter to them, "For I think that God has exhibited us apostles as last of all, like men sentenced to death, because we have become a spectacle to the world, to angels, and to men" (1 Cor. 4:9).

The modern church has a relatively weak angelology, but scripture does not, and neither do some of the greatest thinkers in Christian history.[69] Though the apostles and all followers of Christ frequently face persecution that is visible to others, part of Paul's consolation to us is that we have become spectacles to angels. Though our eyes cannot see, there is a realm of principalities, powers, and forces in "heavenly places" (Eph. 6:12). It is often to this unseen audience that we suffer and glorify Christ.

One of the greatest threats to solid theology is anthropocentrism. God is brought into the drama of the human experience and is the means by which healing and reconciliation of our fallen nature are achieved and gifted to mankind. At the core of history, the pains and pleasures of the present, and the promise of future glory-- humans rest securely as the nucleus. This belief explains the reaction of the Catholic church to Galileo's heliocentric model of the solar system; it also explains our frustration when we don't get what we want or when we don't have a narrative to explain why something is happening to us in particular.

This man-centered view of the world, however, is not the gospel we have received. Throughout scripture, humans are brought into God's grand story, not vice versa. There are several evidences of this.

Recorded history does not begin with humans. By the time God creates Adam, a cosmic drama has already taken place: a war in the heavens over who is most glorified, ending with Satan and his legions cast from heaven for their attempt to usurp God's authority.

It was the hate of God and his glory that caused the serpent to tempt Eve to disobey. Eve is not the intended target, though he takes great pleasure in her pain. She was a pawn in his attempt to rob God of glory.

The promise of a Messiah is first preached not to Adam and Eve but as a curse against Satan, "I will put enmity between you and the woman, and between your offspring and her offspring; he shall bruise your head, and you shall bruise his heel" (Gen. 3:15).

In another instance, Job's righteousness and obedience during persecution are evidenced in an already-occurring audience of heavenly beings. He is both blessed and cursed for God's glory.

Elsewhere, we are told that heavenly beings are watching as God's redemptive plan unfolds and "long to look" to see its fulfillment (1 Pet. 1:12). Indeed, all of Revelation is a play performed before a heavenly audience, with its chief end being God's glorification.

All of our lives, past, present, and future, are lived *coram Deo*.[70] Your blessings and struggles, good and bad, are your invitation into a heavenly drama in which you and I are not the center.

There's something freeing about relinquishing control of *the* story, about stepping out of the limelight and seeing God as sovereign. Make no mistake; you aren't letting God have control; He is in control. You are surrendering to that ocean of love and good purposes not despite deep suffering but because of it and through it.

I bring my patients here regularly. In the pain of depression, while hearing the roar of anxiety, the disorientation of hallucinations or delusions, the taunt of OCD, wounds of trauma, and highs and lows of emotion, we need the stabilizing truth of our sovereign God. He isn't scared, shocked, confused, or uncertain regarding the circumstances of my patient's trial. He lovingly orchestrates all things for our good, though it often doesn't feel that way.

God's Goodness in a World of Suffering

In the lives of those patients I've presented above, we can see God's sovereignty in suffering, that he purposes beautiful things out of ugly situations. We feel good when we see what is broken made into something new. What we don't feel so comfortable with is knowing who has done the breaking. Even more so when proclaiming Him as good while doing it.

From the third century BC, a man named Epicurus raises this objection. He, like others in his day and many today, does not view the glorification of God as our great purpose. In fact, because there is suffering in the world, he used logical proofs to argue that God is *not* good and thus *not* worthy of our worship.

His argument (called the Epicurean Trilemma) is summarized like this:

- If God is willing but unable to prevent suffering/evil, then he is not omnipotent.
- If God is not willing but able to prevent suffering/evil, then he is not benevolent.
- If God is not willing or able to prevent suffering/evil, then why call him God?

Epicurus was a hedonist; he sought pleasure and happiness as his chief aim. It was, for him, the great pursuit of mankind to maximize pleasure and minimize pain. With this goal, why should God be good? Indeed, I agree. If God's ultimate goal for creating this universe was to maximize our pleasure and minimize pain, then I don't think it's shocking to say he failed and is not worthy of being called God. It is revealed that this is the one conclusion that precedes each of Epicurus' premises: that the chief end of God is to create a world with as little suffering as possible. This, though discomforting to say, was not the goal of creation.

If instead of our happiness and pleasure, the goal of the world, the heavens, and everything in existence was not our ultimate happiness and pleasure but the glorification of God's son, Jesus, then by whatever means that occurs most maximally is, by definition, the best world.

We serve a good God in that though there is suffering, we are most abundantly blessed and happy when he is most glorified in us. This is how John Piper, in his work with Desiring God, can call himself a "Christian Hedonist" in that we know the pursuit of God's glory, by whatever means necessary-- suffering included, leads to our greatest satisfaction and pleasure. What a great God we serve in that He has not created

The Mind for His Glory

a world for our pleasure; instead, He has created us for His glory and, in that, ordained that we might be most happy and satisfied in the pursuit.

An ancient art style from Japan called Kintsugi originated in the 15th century, which involves filling the cracks of broken pottery with gold. Instead of hiding the imperfections caused by pieces of broken pottery, this art style accentuates them. The history of the skillful original design, the accidental traumatic breaking, and the artist's repair are evident all in the same piece of pottery. This is a comforting story for many reasons. First, it amplifies the skill of the artist. For those who have tried it, pottery is not as easy as the professionals make it seem. Varying degrees of pressure, moisture, heat, and paint must be applied, or the clay will fracture before completion. The skill of a potter is displayed in its final form.

We are comforted by this story because, though we don't know how the pottery was broken, we can imagine many ways it could happen. After all, evil (chaos) is something we know exists in the world. We see it in our own lives when black ice sends our tires sliding into the rear bumper of the car in front of us, when our anger bubbles over into sharp words, or when sickness strikes our infant child. We imagine the potter's shock when he discovers his hard work cracked and broken.

We also take comfort in the potter's craftiness. We imagine him stooping down to pick up the shards of his creation, collecting them carefully, thinking for a moment, and then placing small ingots of gold into a basin and applying intense heat. Slowly, he pours the gold into the cracks, allowing it to cool at just the right speed so as not to cause more damage.

Our potter is an artisan. Like us, he's subjected to the chaos of living in a fallen world and is crafty in his repairs. We feel good because he looks like us, and we, too, can be artistic and crafty.

The problem with this version is that our potter, though crafty and artistic, lacks something our God has. Our potter is not all-powerful, and therefore, he is not sovereign.

Today, you can buy Kintsugi vases "on demand." Skilled potters delicately work clay on wheels, operate kilns, paint with accuracy, and then lift the item they worked diligently to create and smash it on the ground. Then, they prepare to repair the cracks they just created. Isn't it nonsense?

We know it's not nonsense because the beauty of Kintsugi shows that there's something about the final product that is more beautiful and displays the artist's talent more than before it was broken. The broken and repaired vessel displays the creator's power in a way something unbroken never could.

This potter is in control, not just in the original design but from conception to the finished product. Though we might have found it strange to see him lift the pottery above his head and smash it to the ground, those who knew the plan saw the breaking and knew it (though painful) to ultimately be for the vessel's good and the potter's glory. For some, the presence of suffering means that God isn't good, but we don't see what He is doing. I imagine the marble would curse the sculptor if it felt the chisel.

Not only is our Heavenly Father entirely sovereign, but He is also entirely good. In his plans, in the means he uses to achieve those plans, Dane Ortlund writes, "Seeing God's greatness is not our deepest need, but seeing his goodness."[71] In

Lamentations, we read, "for he does not afflict from his heart or grieve the children of men," so how do we reconcile these two truths? Ortlund writes,

> "The one who rules and ordains all things brings affliction into our lives with a certain divine reluctance. He is not reluctant about the ultimate good that is going to be brought about through that pain; that, indeed, is why he is doing it. But something recoils within him in sending that affliction. The pain itself does not reflect his heart".[72]

Not only is God sovereign, but He is also good. As Joni Eareckson Tada wrote, "God is good not because he gives us answers but because he gives us himself."

Theology and Spiritual Abuse

Before moving forward, it is sadly necessary to confront one of the pitfalls on the road to increased knowledge of God. In a fallen world, we must define and explore the weaponization of doctrine and spiritual abuse. Let it be as a continuation of the doctrine of Total Depravity that the beauty of such theological truths could be manipulated to cause harm.

Years ago, I was asked to write a guidance document for a church on spiritual abuse. Within the church, there was a struggle between differentiating those deconstructing their faith to call adherence to doctrine spiritual abuse and examples of twisting Biblical truth to coerce, subjugate, invalidate, and belittle. The difficulty was not in identifying its impact on those in each group but in fighting to maintain sound doctrine amid this proxy war. Much of what I said in that document could be summarized by A.W. Tozer, "The devil is a better theologian than any of us and a devil still." The harm in doctrine comes not in the doctrine itself but in the sinful heart of man, which applies it.

The fact is that Biblical truth has been weaponized throughout history to oppress, manipulate, and abuse others. Evil has no inspirational or creative potential, forcing it to twist what has been made good. I firmly believe the more potent the good in a doctrine, the more powerfully it can be used to harm.

J.I. Packer said, "A half-truth masquerading as the whole truth becomes a complete untruth." We would be wise to heed this warning as the most powerful weapons used by the enemy take this form. Just enough truth to make us pause and consider, just enough lie to remain undetected, and before long, we have arrived at a disastrous falsehood.

To name some examples, the theology of male headship has been applied not as a means to reflect Christ's leadership and love for the Church but to subjugate women. Kathy Keller said,

> "I will never be one to dismiss or make light of the horrible record of abuse suffered by women at the hands of men who wielded twisted and unbiblical definitions of "headship" and "submission" as their primary weapon. The church should not overlook or minimize one iota of that suffering, but I would beg that we not throw the baby out along with the dirty bathwater. Bail bathwater, by all means available, but save the baby, which in this case is the rightful acceptance of gender roles as Jesus has both defined and embodied them."[73]

Evangelism and the Great Commission became a false banner under which the crusades would commit war crimes. The doctrine of election has induced pride in many rather than a humble reverence. The perseverance of the saints became "eternal security," a license to live wickedly.

The task of Christians pursuing mental wellness for themselves and others is to search diligently for truth, correctly identify falsehoods masquerading as half-truths, and steward the truth we have found wisely, sharing it in love; otherwise, we become "clanging cymbals" (1 Cor. 13:1).

Increased knowledge of God can occasionally lead to another uncomfortably common occurrence in believers' lives. At times, there is a great divide between what we cognitively know to be true and what we feel to be true, and this dissonance can lead to psychological malady.

Felt Truth

Sometimes, we read God's word, filled with incredible promises and provisions, and we pick up books from renowned authors of old, the Apostolic Fathers, the Reformers, and the Puritans, and we are left with a feeling of sadness. Why? One reason is because we may know and affirm what God said, and they have eloquently echoed to be true, but we don't feel it. This is described as a dissonance or "lack of harmony" between what we know and feel. Our heads and hearts might as well be miles apart, which is a profoundly uncomfortable feeling.

Some may read the stories of Christians above, their lives, and God's work through them, but they may feel it can't be true of them personally. Others despair so much of their sin and fallenness that the promises of God, which we all to some degree falsely believe to be dependent on our works, feel to us as a disqualification. If you struggle to feel as true what you know in your head to be true, you are in the company of every other Christian who has ever lived. If instead of feeling hope at the promises of God you despair of your sin, do not fear; the road to the triumph of Romans 8, "There is therefore now no condemnation for those who are in Christ Jesus" (v1), travels through the path of Romans 7, "Wretched man that I am! Who will deliver me from this body of death?" (v24). As Dane

Ortlund says in his book *Deeper: Real Change for Real Sinners*, "One reason some Christians remain shallow their whole lives is they do not allow themselves ever more deeply throughout their lives, to pass through the painful corridor of honesty about who they really are."[74]

Much of mental health trial comes by believing lies or struggling to believe the truth. We see this when a patient believes lies spoken to her about her value or worth in an abusive relationship. When patients feel there is no hope as they confront a difficult diagnosis. When adolescents tell themselves they aren't worthy because they don't look like, act like, or believe what those around them do,

The difficult knowledge patients come to understand is that it is only *through* struggle (experienced for oneself or on behalf of another) that head knowledge can become heart knowledge. This is the "tested genuineness of your faith" (1 Pet. 1:7-9). Untested knowledge is not worthless, but it is of much lesser worth than knowledge that has stood the trials of life to become a bedrock foundation on which to build our work for the Kingdom. My encouragement to patients is threefold: first, confront the lies that have been spoken to you from within and without. Second, do not despise the testing of one's faith. Cling firmly to what you *know* to be true, and by God's grace, he progressively moves what is known to be what is *felt*. Third, realize that it is not the *feeling* that proves a truth to be true, to reject the idea that feelings are the litmus test for truth, and when felt truth is experienced, it is a gift, not a requirement for true faith.

Truth Lived Out

The essence of Cognitive Behavioral Therapy is that how we think, act, and feel influence one another. Changing behavior can change our thoughts and emotions; similarly, changing thoughts can change our behavior and emotions as well. In many ways, our behavior is evidence of what we think and believe. For example, sitting in a chair is a conscious or unconscious assent to the chair's ability to support our weight.

We put a lot of weight into feelings. We assume that feelings are the greatest test of what we believe. But what if they aren't? What if what we do and how we act is a better indication of what we believe than what we feel? Do you want to know what someone believes? Look at their behavior.

How do you know you believe in God? Do you pray? The Bible tells us, "Whoever would draw near to God must believe that he exists, and that he rewards those who seek him." (Heb. 11:6)

Do you trust God? Look at behavior; despite anxiety, do you do what he has called you to do? Do you believe Jesus is the Christ? Do you stand up for Him as His ambassador on earth? (Matt. 10:33). Do you know you are a Christ follower? "Whoever says 'I know him' but does not keep his commandments is a liar, and the truth is not in him... whoever says he abides in him ought to walk in the same way in which he walked" (1 John 2:4-5).

It can be scary to look at our behavior to determine our beliefs. Behavior is hard, and talk is cheap. It's much easier to say "Lord, Lord" than follow Him daily. Because of this, to many, he will say, " I never knew you." (Matt. 7:22-23).

This is not works-based righteousness. It is looking at a duck and expecting it to quack. As we will discuss later, it is going to an apple tree and expecting apples or to the fig tree and expecting figs. Do you wonder what you believe? Not just what you confess, think, or feel, but what you truly believe? Look at your behavior.

This transformation from head knowledge into a living and active faith is part of a process that takes place throughout the entirety of the Christian walk. It is brought about through the trials and hardships along the way; as George Müller said, "Faith grows with use." It is not linear, and it is not easy, but it is part of being made into the likeness of Christ. As we grow in our knowledge of God, our goal is to become more like Him, the topic of our next chapter.

CHAPTER 4

…BE CONFORMED INTO THE LIKENESS OF HIS SON…

"If all that I meet / shall turn to my good / the bitter is sweet, / the medicine food; / though painful at present / 'twill cease before long, / and then, O how pleasant / the conqueror's song!"

JOHN NEWTON

I have often wondered what it would have been like to follow Jesus when he walked the earth. Given the gospel reports, I suspect it would have been very difficult. The frequent travel, uncertain food supply, and stormy seas may have caused some discomfort, but we don't hear of disciples leaving Jesus because of these things. We see many readily dispensing of earthly pleasures to follow Him. Over and above the hardships they faced, what made it difficult to follow Jesus and caused others to leave was the difficulty of his preaching (John 6:66).[75] Take, for example, the instructions in the greatest sermon preached on earth, the Sermon on the Mount.

Even in its blessings, we are called to a painful self-reflection in the Beatitudes. Who is poor in spirit, mourning, meek, hungering for righteousness, merciful and pure in heart, a peacemaker and persecuted for righteousness but Him? (Matt. 5:1-12). Who can fulfill the demands of his teaching on anger, lust, divorce, oaths, and loving enemies? (Matt. 5:21-48). For as much as Puritan preachers' sermons brought fire-and-brimstone conviction, none could convict as much as the words spoken from this blessed Mount. Here, the law is given, which echoes and amplifies the requirements given to Moses on Mount Sinai. For "…unless your righteousness surpasses that of the Pharisees and the teachers of the law, you will certainly not enter the kingdom of heaven." (Matt. 5:20). We could not hope to uphold that one, much less this one which concerns itself with actions and the orientations of the heart.

In his preaching, Jesus holds himself up as the standard against which we will be judged, as the perfect example of the law lived out. It is a fearful thing to compare ourselves to Christ. As our measuring stick, we fall hopelessly short.

Yet, He has provided us with help through His Spirit, poured out on all believers and tasked with bringing about the changing work of conformity into the likeness of our Savior. We call this process sanctification, which will not be complete until we pass away or He returns.

It is the work of the Holy Spirit in the lives of believers we discuss in this chapter. He holds the chisel, and Jesus serves as the model as He removes those elements that do not reflect the Son. His work is not just in the negative, for it was His coming, which would also be additive in the lives of Christians, clothing them in "power from on high" (Luke 24:49).

The impact of conformity into the likeness of Christ on psychology rests in, first, our relationship to this difficult process called sanctification, namely that we believe the root of and sustaining work is given by the Holy Spirit but calls us to work out this salvation in "fear and trembling." Second, our becoming like Christ changes how we interact with one another relationally. Truly, we are called individually to the cross but stand before it as a part of a new family, in a relationship with one another stronger and more powerful than filial kinship; this is the Body we call the Church. Third, it changes how we are seen by the world, who curiously look in to see Christians interacting with one another and with the outside world in a way that confounds earthly sense.

Fear and Trembling

The concept of salvation *sola gratia*, by grace alone, independent of our worthiness or work, is what makes our gospel so good. God did not look at the lives of His people and see any goodness that caused his sovereign choice, nor does his salvation require that believers perform works to keep this free gift of grace. The grace that saves is the same that sustains, and both come from above. It is to this beautiful picture of love and mercy that the book of James may catch us off guard. Before we address the seeming contradiction of the theology of works James presents, let us examine the thoughts of early Christians regarding the gospel message.

By around 55AD, the gospel had spread far across the eastern continent of Europe. Paul had silenced a poisonous thought from Rome: if God is glorified as He redeems sinners, shall we purposely sin so that His glory increases? Paul's response was swift, "By no means! How can we who died to sin still live in it? Do you not know that all of us who have been baptized into Christ Jesus were baptized into his death? We were buried therefore with him by baptism into death, in order that, just as Christ was raised from the dead by the glory of the Father, we too might walk in newness of life" (Rom. 6:3-6). Earlier in his letter to the Galatian Christians, he had proclaimed freedom from the law, "For freedom Christ has set us free; stand firm therefore, and do not submit again to a yoke of slavery" (5:1). Now he proclaims freedom from another yoke, that of slavery to sin.

Paul's message is twofold: We have been freed from the demands of the law by the one who fulfilled them perfectly so that we may walk in newness of life, and we have died to sin and been raised with Christ. We are freed from obligation to the law and freed from slavery to sin. There are no humans who walk the earth more freely than the Christians.[76]

James addresses these freed Christians, "What good is it, my brothers, if someone says he has faith but does not have works? Can that faith save him?" (James 2:14). The answer is no, *that* faith cannot save a soul. The faith found in *sola fide* is not a faith that responds as James illustration shows, "If a brother or sister is poorly clothed and lacking in daily food, and one of you says to them, 'Go in peace, be warmed and filled,' without giving them the things needed for the body, what good is that?" (v16). Ours is not a faith of empty words and promises but a faith of obedience and action, "So also faith by itself, if it does not have works, is dead" (v17). James points us to a faith that is active and evidenced by works, not a faith that is born or secured by works. Martin Luther said, "justification is by faith alone, but not by a faith that is alone."

We may look at this relationship between faith and works like a tree and fruit. Is an apple tree an apple tree before it produces apples? Yes. Is the presence of an apple what makes it an apple tree? In one sense, no, but something should cause serious pause regarding the health and identity of a tree that is called an apple tree that bears no apples. More thoroughly, if an apple tree never produced fruit, an argument could be made that it shouldn't be called an apple tree. In taxonomy, it may be classified as an apple tree, but functionally, it didn't perform as apple trees do; we may consider it "dead," as James did faith without works.

Later, in Paul's letter to the Philippians, he echoes James, "Therefore, my beloved, as you have always obeyed, so now, not only as in my presence but much more in my absence, work out your own salvation with fear and trembling" (2:13).

Again, the crushing weight of obedience seems to fall on the Christian, but Praise God Paul doesn't end with verse 13. He continues, "for it is God who works in you, both to will and to work for his good pleasure" (v13). The grace that saves and sustains is also the grace that leads us into progressive obedience to Christ, all of which comes from God for his good pleasure.

James concurs, "But [God] gives more grace. Therefore it says, 'God opposes the proud but gives grace to the humble.' Submit yourselves therefore to God" (James 4:6-7a) and again, "Draw near to God, and he will draw near to you" (v8) and, "Humble yourselves before the Lord, and he will exalt you" (v10). Faithful action and obedience draw their strength from God, not the believer.

Without this unified view, the psychology of the believer is prone to disorder. A theology of faith without works is prone to apathy. It ultimately threatens to coddle the unredeemed into a false sense of security regarding the state of their soul before God. A works-based righteousness, or one that originates within the believer's heart, can cause anxiety, shame, and discouragement. Only faith working itself out in love, originating and sustained by the grace of God, can produce an active and lively faith free of the crushing standard of righteousness and holiness required.

Sin has a profound impact on mental health. It has painful natural consequences, and our loving Father disciplines us when we are in the wrong so that we may stay close to Him on the narrow road. I have seen many instances of sin impacting mental health. The man, in an active affair, who struggles with insomnia and anxiety, who mistakes the conviction of the Holy Spirit for a psychological problem. The person with narcissistic personality traits who abuses others finds themselves ever more isolated and alone. The young man stuck in cycles of addiction who finds themselves spiraling deeper into depression which only worsens the desire for the use of substances as a maladaptive coping skill. There are many more examples.

The world would have us believe that our pursuit of right living and avoidance of sin is bondage, that the choice to do whatever one wants, whenever one wants, is the greatest form of self-expression and freedom. But do their lives evidence human flourishing? Do they have peace and joy amid the most challenging circumstances? Beyond all the talk of freedom to do whatever one pleases, does the evidence suggest they are truly living their best life?

To say God cannot sin is not a restriction of His power. To sin is to place oneself in bondage, to limit oneself, something God logically cannot do. Our loving God does not give us commands against sin because He wishes to restrict us. He desires that we would be more free. Adam and Eve were most free when they lived in the garden with only one command. Our sin placed us in bondage that only the very death of God could undo.

We are called not to be slaves to sin but to righteousness (Rom. 6:21). This is when we are most mentally well. Conformity to Christlikeness has massive implications for our mental health.

So the weight of a yoke of obedience we could never carry rests on our shoulders, but to our surprise, it is easy and light. Why? Because the one who fulfilled the law and set us free from its demands, the penalty of sin, and death, Jesus Christ, stands beside you, bearing the weight and enabling your every step forward. So plant your feet firmly into the ground and run the race set before you so that you may receive the crown and say as Paul did, "I have fought the good fight, I have finished the race, I have kept the faith" (2 Tim. 4:7).

Obedience out of Fear or Love

For some, the section above will have caused anxiety. Some see their failings and just as quickly see the justice and righteousness of God and are filled with fear. As I have observed in the clinic, it seems this is often due to our upbringing. We all fall somewhere between overemphasis and underemphasis of God's justice and mercy. It is right and good to understand God as simultaneously just and merciful, but when it comes to pursuing obedience, I know most certainly that obedience out of fear is nowhere as effective as obedience out of love. If we want to live a life conformed to the likeness of Christ, we need an affection to fill our hearts to a greater degree than Earth's shallow wells ever could.

A story was told by a physics professor who tasked his students with removing all the air inside a large glass jar. Dutifully, his students set to work devising pumps, vacuums, and meters, all to both remove and confirm the removal of the air from inside this jar. After their work was complete and several impressive, albeit expensive, devices sat in front of him, the professor asked, "What if I told you I could do what you did more effectively, more quickly, and at a fraction of the cost?" The students laughed, assured they had come up with the only and best way to accomplish the task. The smiling professor took a large pitcher of water from underneath the table and poured its contents into the glass jar until it overflowed onto the floor. The air had been removed from the container. The principle is that it is harder to eliminate air by removing it directly than it is to remove it by filling the space with something else.

Often, Christians come to my practice seeking to rid their lives of some known sin. They are frustrated by its continual tempting presence and seek to rid themselves of it. Many have spent time contemplating the justice of God and pairing sin against the divine hammer of judgment until they are consumed by fear and guilt. In these instances, the desire for something sinful has been replaced by fear of punishment. This, time proves, is not a powerful enough stimulus. The only stimulus powerful enough to rid us of one desire is the expulsive power of a greater desire. A concept explored by Thomas Chalmers in his book, *The Expulsive Power of a New Affection*.

Take the patient who struggles with the powerful supranormal stimulus of pornography. They have tried for years to stop yielding to the temptation. When asked how they combat the desire to watch pornography, they usually say something to the effect of "I usually wait for the desire to pass." This is foolish! First, we must remove the environment and preconditions for viewing it. Sitting on the couch "waiting for it to pass" is hardly effective. This tactic alone, however, is rarely enough. Secondly and more importantly, we must love something more than it. Not just any "it" either, something which satisfies to a greater extent than the shallow well of pornography ever could. Chalmers said, "The love of the world cannot be expunged by a mere demonstration of the world's worthlessness. But may it not be supplanted by the love of that which is more worthy than itself?"[77]

For non-Christians, I encourage them to turn to goal-directed activities that move them toward a fruitful and effective life, such as exercise, socialization, education, and creativity, among others. For Christians, I can similarly point to these activities but with the natural and effective end of glorifying the one person whose love and affection supplant any earthly love. This simultaneously removes preconditions for temptation while also pointing our hearts toward the object of our ultimate desire, Jesus.

Most encouragingly, the love of Jesus to which we apply our affection is displayed by a gospel that turned ordinary Kingship on its head. We have been conquered by a Lord who did so not that we may languish under his oppressive hand or who desires to remove any pleasurable thing from our lives that we may be miserable, but that we might be freed slaves of Righteousness. We will explore this transformative gospel next.

A Servant King

Just as quickly as humans began gathering together in tribes and clans, leaders began to emerge to ensure order and execute justice. Whether they went by the name of tribal chiefs, feudal lords, warrior kings, or emperors, these leaders could be distinguished from their subjects by many factors: their wealth, access to resources, and the respect offered or commanded by them. Yet no other factor distinguished a king from his subjects more than dominance over their enemies. To consolidate power, kings through history murdered families, torched villages, and took prisoners to exert their authority. No method was more successful in showing a conqueror's victory over the conquered than lifting the victim impaled on a stake or hanging them from a tree or tower to show everyone (both friend and foe) the extent of force a king would take to acquire and maintain power.

Along the road to many kingdoms throughout history were the traitors of the king, enemies of the kingdom, and threats to power; you may have seen their bodies impaled and left to suffer for hours or days before succumbing to blood loss, dehydration, suffocation, or shock. Along with physical torment, these enemies of the king faced the jeers of fearful subjects, eager to show anyone around whose side they were on, certainly not the side of one who hung from the tree, lest they find themselves beside them in agony.

The Jewish people, who had awaited a coming Messiah with great expectancy, had, in many ways, grown sleepy with time. Like the women in Matthew 25:1, who, while waiting for the coming groom, took their lamps but failed to take oil with them and fell asleep in the darkness of the extinguished light.

Unsurprisingly, a baby born in the lowliest of places failed to wake them from their slumber. Instead, the inauguration of the Kingdom of our LORD and of his Christ was preached not to the religious elite but to the only ones awake and watching, pagan Wise Men and shepherds awake at night tending their flock. The one who would triumphantly restore order as kings of history have for centuries tried was born and placed in a feeding trough.

As the young Messiah grows, He aligns himself not with the political elite nor with the wealthy or powerful. His closest companions are tax collectors, fishermen, and prostitutes formerly possessed by demons, and more than this, he travels, dines, and lodges with the detestable and often ridicules the religious leaders for their wealth and supposed piety.

This same Christ instructs his disciples to adopt the mindset of a little child rather than that of a warrior, priest, or sage. He likens them to sheep, the most foolish of the livestock, and says that when persecuted or reviled, they should pray for their enemies.

Instead of commanding others to care for his needs, to give him money, food, and status, he feeds his disciples, going so far as to invite them to eat of his very body, drink his blood, and then he washes their feet. By the standard of kings, it is as if he read the rulebook and set out to do everything perfectly opposite.

In this King of King's death, the wisdom of the world and the way of conquering kings of old is turned completely on its head. Here, on the cross, the one to whom every knee would bow and every mouth confess as Lord is lifted like the treasonous prisoners of secular kings. It would not have been easy for anyone in that time to accept Jesus as "The King of the Jews," let alone King of Kings. He hung there as many before had who threatened the earthly power of Ceasar and the State. To the people, His being lifted up on the cross was evidence He was no king at all.

Yet our King Jesus is lifted up again while on the earth, this time not in shame but in glory, calling all people to himself in his resurrection. Jesus proves He is not just the rightful King of the Jews or of the Earth but over death itself.

When we look back on this God-man's life, we might assume that at this point, His kingdom is inaugurated, the resurrection. No, the kingdom was in the manger, at the table with sinners, instructing children, washing feet, and lifted up on a cross. This is a kingdom unlike any other on the earth. It's a kingdom on its head.

Herman Bavinck says,

> "The Kingdom of God will in the true, full sense be a dominion, but that dominion will be a human dominion, the dominion of the Son of man. And thus Jesus now also says that He most certainly is a King, the King of Israel, the King promised and anointed of God. But He is that nevertheless in a sense different from the one the Jews entertain. He is a King who rides on a colt, the foal of an ass, a King of righteousness and peace, a King who is also Priest, a King who is also Savior. Might and love, righteousness and grace, exaltation and humility, God and man are conjoined in Him."[78]

So also A.W. Tozer writes of our response to Christ's example,

> "The Christian soon learns that if he would be victorious as a son of heaven among men on earth he must not follow the common pattern of mankind, but rather the contrary. That he may be safe he puts himself in jeopardy; he loses his life to save it and is in danger of losing it if he attempts to preserve it. He goes down to get up. If he refuses to go down he is already down, but when he starts down he is on his way up. He is strongest when he is weakest and weakest when he is strong. Though poor he has the power to make

others rich, but when he becomes rich his ability to enrich others vanishes. He has most after he has given most away and has least when he possesses most. He may be and often is highest when he feels lowest and most sinless when he is most conscious of sin. He is wisest when he knows that he knows not and knows least when he has acquired the greatest amount of knowledge. He sometimes does most by doing nothing and goes furthest when standing still. In heaviness he manages to rejoice and keeps his heart glad even in sorrow. The paradoxical character of the Christian is revealed constantly."[79]

In terms of kings and kingdoms, servant leadership, as displayed by Christ, is an anomaly, more than an outlier. In terms of deity, it's nonsensical. A brief examination of the myths of ancient Greece or Rome, or further back of Babylonian or Mesopotamian texts, reveals the role of the gods as divine creators, yet to sustain what is created falls almost universally on the shoulders of humans through servitude. Pastor and Theologian Michael Reeves said, "Have you ever thought about the gods of human religion? All of them share something in common: they are needy. They need us to serve or worship them; they're weak…. So why would god create the world? To get some friends; to get some slaves? See such a god needs us. His glory is like a black hole sucking in—taking."[80]

Take the Babylonian god Marduk, who establishes order from chaos and assumes his place as head among all gods. After his peace is established, he creates humans and leads them captive in his train to indefinite involuntary servitude.

Or take the Greek myths, rife with shapeshifting deities who use their powers to rape and exploit humans. Time doesn't permit us to discuss Zeus' torture of Prometheus, who gave fire to mankind, and his wife Hera's fury at Io, who Zeus turned into a heifer. The unfair punishment of Medusa (formerly a mortal) who Poseidon raped. The evidence of the fall is deep in the mythology of these ancient (and modern) cultures.

Marduk leads captives in his train to servitude. Jesus leads captives in his train to freedom, "For freedom Christ has set us free…" (Gal. 5:1). God gives us work to do, but not so that he can do nothing, but so that we might take part in his redemptive work, alongside Him, "My Father is working until now, and I am working" (John 5:17).

So what is a follower of this King Jesus to look like? In being conformed into His likeness we find ourselves in the posture of a servant. Jesus instructs his disciples, "You know that the rulers of the Gentiles lord it over them, and their great ones exercise authority over them. It shall not be so among you. But whoever would be great among you must be your servant, and whoever would be first among you must be your slave, even as the Son of Man came not to be served but to serve, and to give his life as a ransom for many" (Matt. 20:25-28). Herman Bavinck describes it this way, "True, He constantly exhibited His royal power, but He exhibited it not in a show of dominion as the rulers of the nations did, but in serving and in giving His soul as a ransom for many."[81]

The fallen human psychology is filled with a desire for lordship. We may not consciously think it, but we crave the power, prestige, and control that it produces. So, as we fail to grasp this control or grasp it to incomplete degrees, we find ourselves anxious, depressed, ruminating, and ashamed. What if, instead, we surrendered to the Kingdom of Christ and assumed the posture he modeled for us on earth? Might we be freed, to some degree, from the anxiety of wanting more or fearing to lose? Could some of the things that lead us to depression, feeling forgotten, betrayed, or alone, be instead evidence that we are walking in the steps of our Savior who so often was in that same place in a world that so routinely rejected him?

The servant leadership relationship that Jesus demonstrated was meant to be lived out among the members of His body, the Church. When non-Christians look into our congregations, they should see Christians living radically different lives in relation to one another and the world.

Spiritual Gifts and the Fellowship of Believers

As much as this chapter is about conformity into the likeness of Christ, it is inseparably related to how we interact as the Church. Jesus prayed that believers "will all be one" (John 17:21). In one sense, there is no such thing as individual conformity into the likeness of Christ as there is our mutual conformity, "If one member suffers, all suffer together; if one member is honored, all rejoice together" (1 Cor. 12:26). So inseparable is Christ from His body, the Church, that he proclaims Saul's persecution of Christians as persecution of Himself (Acts 9:4).

Similarly Revelation paints a picture of a glorified body of believers more than individual glory (Rev. 7:9) and Jesus praise and admonitions to the churches are spoken of to the whole, "But I have this against *you*, that you have abandoned the love you had at first" (Rev. 2:4, emphasis mine).

As discussed in previous chapters, the Christian road is filled with hardships, trials, and temptations. Our good God has given us many gifts along the way. Though some (such as those of modern medicine and psychology) fall like rain on the just and unjust (Matt. 5:45), there is a gift He has given only to believers who have received Jesus in faith: membership in a local church.

In the darkest times, the apostles looked to the fellowship of the saints for comfort, provision, and support. When Paul needed support, he called for Timothy to come quickly (2 Tim. 4:21). So, too, as we experience suffering, our local church and global family are here to support us, and we support them. Indeed, one of the reasons we experience trials is that we may help others when they experience something similar (2 Cor. 1:4). Dietrich Bonhoeffer explains it well in his book *Life Together*,

> "It is true, of course, that what is an unspeakable gift of God for the lonely individual is easily disregarded and trodden under foot by those who have the gift every day. It is easily forgotten that the fellowship of Christian brethren is a gift of grace, a gift of the Kingdom of God that any day may be taken from us, that the time that still separates us from utter loneliness may be brief indeed. Therefore, let him who until now has had the privilege of living a common Christian life with other Christians praise God's grace from the bottom of his heart. Let him thank God on his knees and declare: It is grace, nothing but grace, that we are allowed to live in community with Christian brethren."

While Bonhoffer's description is certainly more than church attendance on a Sunday, it isn't less.

Unfortunately, this is not everyone's experience of the Church. Rather than treating one another as living individual members of our own body and that of Christ Himself, we more often look and behave exactly like the world.

Living in Christian community is hard work because the closer we grow together the more our fallenness becomes apparent to the fellowship of believers. We are being formed into the likeness of Christ by one another, and that's hard work. Mark Dever writes,

"I often hear Christians talking about their different spiritual gifts. Yet I wonder how often people consider the fact that God has given so many gifts precisely so that those gifts might be used in response to the sin of other Christians in the church. My sins give you a chance to exercise your gifts."[82]

Behaving as the church should is only possible through the work of the Holy Spirit, who gives these gifts so that we may live and serve one another.

Many try to figure out what *specific* spiritual gifts they have been gifted with. There are paper tests and online quizzes. Instead, John Piper states, "I really believe that the problem of not knowing our spiritual gifts is not a basic problem. More basic is the problem of not desiring very much to strengthen other people's faith."[83] Paul writes of his desire to visit the Roman church, "For I long to see you, that I may impart to you some spiritual gift to strengthen you—that is, that we may be mutually encouraged by each other's faith, both yours and mine" (Ro. 1:11-12). How do you best serve the Church? How do you best serve individual church members? In what area of ministry do you feel like you fit the role much like a glove fits a hand? Perhaps it isn't this strong of a fit, in which case we start with what areas you are especially thankful that someone else is gifted to serve in that way?[84]

Equipping

When my younger sister moved with her husband into a new house shortly after the birth of their first child, there was a lot of work to be done. First, the moving itself was made exponentially more complex by my infant nephew and his many supplies. In addition there was painting, drywalling, and electrical wiring to be done. I was home in the Midwest and supporting them through the process. We tried our hardest not to feel the encroaching spirit of hopelessness as we recognized our lack of equipping for the tasks ahead. Just when we felt the last rays of hope drain from our bodies, a train of cars pulled into the driveway. Friends from my family's local church pulled in, many of whom I recognized. An older friend who worked for years placing drywall, one who I knew worked as an electrician, their wives to watch my nephew, another bringing food, and about ten able-bodied college men to help me and my brother-in-law lift heavy things. I smiled, seeing this Christian community using their skills to help. Each had been uniquely equipped to assist.

The work of unique giftings within the body doesn't stop at home construction and moving. Other trials experienced by the body may require those who know the requirements of serving children with disabilities to assist new parents after the birth of their child, another who feels at home in the medical setting providing hospital room prayers, or those who can process complex grief and bereavement supporting someone facing profound loss. There is a very real sense in which the care of a member experiencing a mental health crisis is a church-wide effort.

We have discussed previously how our sufferings help us serve others when they are struggling, and so, too, the often confusing, circuitous path of training on which God takes us. We can't say for sure, but I'm fairly sure there came a time in Paul's missionary journey when his tent-making skills were exactly what was needed. Did Matthew help balance the disciple's books because of his work as a tax collector, or did Peter give instructions on where the ideal fishing spots were on the Sea of Galilee? Though the plan for each of these disciples, and for Jesus Himself, was set before the foundations of the world, God still had Paul learn of tents, Matthew of money, Peter of fishing, and Jesus of carpentry. So, too, your work in any number of positions you feel are unrelated to the place you'd like to see yourself.

Being conformed into the likeness of Christ means we do not despise the times we are being trained up in areas that may seem unrelated to our vocational aspirations. Instead, we thank God for the opportunity to serve Him in this particular way and at this particular time and ask for opportunities to use those skills in ways we may not anticipate in the future. As Zechariah encouraged those looking at the much smaller rebuilding of the much grander Temple Solomon built, "Whoever has despised the day of small things shall rejoice" (Zech. 4:10). Why? Because that small thing isn't small in God's grand plan.

Fruit of the Spirit

Do you remember the story of Jesus cursing the fig tree? I think we all may find it a little odd reading it. I recently recalled this passage while walking through an orchard in Michigan. Row after row, I'd approach the different types of apples and feel the weight of the branches. Each was heavy with giant bright red and green apples. But it was the time for apples, so I wasn't surprised. Jesus, however, looks for figs when "it was not the season for figs" (Mark 11:13). As a child I felt bad for the tree. There are many different explanations for why Jesus would look for figs when they weren't in season, some pointing to a particular variety of figs that produces in another season, what is clear is that Jesus wants his disciples to see that carrying the outward appearance of a functioning fig tree (leaves, healthy branches, trunk, and roots) but lacking what all of those things are meant for (producing fruit) is unacceptable.

The fruit of the spirit has an immediately apparent twofold

ministry. First, it allows for a functioning body of believers, and it distinguishes Christians from non-Christians

Just as spiritual gifts are necessary for the life of the Church, so too the Fruit of the Spirit is necessary for fallen but redeemed humans to exist in community with one another. Imagine a fellowship without love, joy, peace, forbearance, kindness, goodness, faithfulness, gentleness, and self-control. It would be Pandemonium.[85] What can love, joy, and peace do for human psychology? What can it not do? The Fruit of The Spirit exists not only in pleasant times but as bulwarks of godliness in the hardest times. As Elisabeth Elliot said, "The secret is Christ in me, not me in a different set of circumstances." We may not always be anxiety or depression-free, but we can ask that God continue to grow in us the Fruit that brings a piece of heaven into the Valley of the Shadow of Death, here and now.

Christians are set apart from the world by displaying the fruit of the Spirit: "You will recognize them by their fruits. Are grapes gathered from thornbushes, or figs from thistles?" (Matt. 7:16).

The Communicable Attributes of God

Christians treat each other differently; this alone leads the world to wonder what it is about these people. They also behave differently towards the world. Tim Keller said,

> "The early church was strikingly different from the culture around it in this way - the pagan society was stingy with its money and promiscuous with its body. A pagan gave nobody their money and practically gave everybody their body. And the Christians came along and gave practically nobody their body, and they gave practically everybody their money."

The Roman Emperor Julian, discouraged by the advance of

Christianity in the empire, wrote in a letter,

> "[Christianity] has been specially advanced through the loving service rendered to strangers, and through their care for the burial of the dead. It is a scandal that there is not a single Jew who is a beggar, and that the godless Galileans care not only for their own poor but for ours as well; while those who belong to us look in vain for the help that we should render them."

This is because we possess God's communicable attributes. More than others, we should pursue justice, love mercy, and seek wisdom in matters of church and state. We show justice because the source of all justice lives within us. The same is true for mercy and wisdom, among other things.

We fight for the oppressed, care for widows and orphans, abhor racism, and seek restitution for wrongs done. When wronged, we show mercy; when struck, we turn the other cheek. We forgive not just once but as long and as often as genuine repentance is present.

Human psychology's effectual end is the glorification of God. For the Christian, that process exists in the often painful chiseling into the likeness of Christ. Just as a multitude of temporal problems find their answer in right knowledge of God, so too right living as a body of believers looks progressively more like what it will appear as in heaven as Christians display the servant leadership Christ modeled, use their gifting and equipping to benefit the body and grow in the Fruit of the Spirit. Functioning in this way, we find a kind of fellowship that confronts a loneliness epidemic, the roots of addiction in isolation, and is freed from the shackles of material possessions in generously giving, among a hundred other applications to human psychology.

Adam O'Neill

CHAPTER 5

...TO BECOME MORE EFFECTIVE FOR THE KINGDOM...

> *"Modern Christians hope to save the world by being like it, but it will never work. The Church's power over the world springs out of her unlikeness to it, never from her integration into it."*
>
> AW TOZER

Christians, as discussed in the previous chapter, look different from the world (or at least they should). The radical life Christian's live together, as well as the way they interact with the world at large, inevitably spills into an effectiveness for the fruitful spread of the gospel. In this chapter, we discuss some of the main reasons Christians remain ineffective in their work for the Kingdom: busyness, apathy, regret, and anxiety, among others. What we desire is effectiveness in the present moment.

Effectiveness in the present is about being mindful of a reality we often neglect: our standing in Christ. Being present with hope is looking to our future, which is also here now, a concept we discussed in greater detail in Chapter 2, described as the "already and not yet" of our gospel. Far from realizing this present reality, we spend most of our time either dwelling in the past, ruminating with anxious anticipation of the future, or purposeless in-effectivity in the present.

We owe this aspect of human cognition to the blessing and curse of having a highly evolved frontal lobe. The frontal lobe is where the highest-order thinking occurs and what separates our brains and their capabilities from those of other species. The blessing and curse of this higher-level cognition is the ability to project into the future and craft alternate series of events in the past. Dogs do not create future fiction to worry about, nor do they analyze the past to create alternate endings different from what has occurred; we do, however.[86]

Living in the Past

Regret is a powerful emotion that derives its strength from the concepts of lost time and shame over past mistakes. Regret is akin to grief in many ways. Grief is a result of loss, and regret is the loss of what *could have been*. In addition to feeling bad about what *has* happened (what we may describe as guilt), we also confront what could have happened instead, consciously or unconsciously. Using an example of harsh words spoken to a friend after a conflict, we first lament the hurtful things we said. We acknowledge how it may have caused pain, sometimes lasting, in our friend. Then, we confront how we might have responded differently and the good it could have produced. Responding rightly would have displayed great integrity, perhaps grown the relationship, or produced greater trust and affection. We rightly feel guilt when we do wrong;

this is a gift of God, produced by the Holy Spirit to call us to greater sanctification. Guilt, however, turns to regret when we create these fictional worlds that might have been.

Regret, however, is a denial of God's sovereign plan and his promise to work all things for the good of those who are called according to His purpose (Rom. 8:28). There is no lost time in the eyes of an all-powerful, sovereign God who is working all things for our good and His glory. This does not mean, however, that we should not feel guilty for doing wrong. Suggesting otherwise is similar to the Corinthians' misunderstanding of Grace, "Are we to continue in sin that grace may abound?" (Rom. 6:1). Paul's response is, "By no means!" (Rom. 6:2). Yet, when we do sin, we have the promise of a faithful God, for, "Who shall bring any charge against God's elect? It is God who justifies" (Rom. 8:33). The power of God's divine plan which is unfolding each day does not hang on the balance of your perfect obedience.[87] There is no lost time.

Living in the Future

It seems harsh to begin a section on anxious anticipation of the future with a chastisement. This is because behind every racing heart, palpitation, shaking, and sweating episode is a person who is suffering, and God's heart toward them is love, "For he does not afflict from his heart or grieve the children of men" (Lam. 3:33). Yet the role of the Christian mental health professional is filled with difficult questions, and to this day the one I have had the most discomfort answering for a patient is, "Is anxiety sin?". It is uncomfortable to answer because anxiety is biologically normal for humans living in a fallen world. Yet, simultaneously, we can proclaim that what is normal in a fallen world is not always right nor the way things are destined to be. It is also uncomfortable because I think we all know the answer intrinsically. Behind anxiety are two key elements that are identified in scripture as sinful: arrogance and distrust of a sovereign God.

Arrogance. Anxiety doesn't feel arrogant at all. I know that from personal experience. Anxiety seems to cut us down and make us feel small and unsafe.

The person who is at peace resembles what the psalmist describes in Psalm 131, "But I have calmed and quieted my soul, like a weaned child with its mother; like a weaned child is my soul within me" (v2). A weaned child sits in his mother's lap because he knows what is needed will be provided. He trusts. This is how we are invited to approach our Heavenly Father, like children (Matt. 18:3). The truth is we don't trust God; we trust ourselves.

When we closely examine anxiety, roots of arrogance begin to appear.

We see ourselves as the decider of both what we need and the means of acquiring it, "It is in vain that you rise up early and go late to rest, eating the bread of anxious toil; for he gives to his beloved sleep" (Ps. 127:2). It is God who decides what is needed and grants what is required. John Newton said, "Everything is necessary that he sends you, nothing can be necessary that he withholds from you."

I've seen myself and my heart of arrogant anxiety in my young family members around the holidays. A cousin attempted to carry a hot cup of cocoa to his seat one Christmas, "Let me help you take that to your chair; it's very hot." "No!" he cried,

"I've got it". Though my heart for him was only love, in his eyes, he saw only fear of loss and his profound trust in himself. *What if he takes it from me and doesn't give it back? I don't want to be separated from this good thing for even a moment. I'm more than capable. I've never spilled before.* He sounds just like me; I do that with my work, money, friends, health, and future. *Don't take my money from me, God, I know what to do with it. If I give you my friends, what if you don't return them? If I allow you to control my future, it won't look like I want it to.* Knowing what would follow my cousin's bold trek from the kitchen to the chair, I preemptively grabbed the paper towel and washcloth.

If we look closely, we may also find that what we are striving and anxious for no longer exists in the realm of need but in the realm of want or desire. Aside from ingratitude, this anxious toiling assumes a future we are not guaranteed. It is the farmer in Jesus' parable who had more than enough food in his barns, so he began to build bigger ones, to which God said, "Fool! This night your soul is required of you, and the things you have prepared, whose will they be?'" (Luke 12:20). Instead of this, Jesus asks us to consider the sparrows who neither, "sow nor reap nor gather into barns, and yet your heavenly Father feeds them" (Matt. 6:26).

We find that after we clear away the roots of arrogance in our worry, what remains is a fundamental distrust in our Father. We cannot affirm Jesus' question about birds, "Are you not of more value than they?"

Distrust. So much time is spent living in catastrophic future possibilities. Minds race with endless iterations of traumatic events, great deals of anxiety are felt solving countless problems that will never arise, having conversations that never end up happening, releasing elevated levels of epinephrine, norepinephrine, and cortisol to help our bodies prepare for bodily harm that will never occur.

Yet, how often have I heard that when whatever difficulty arrives (and it is rarely what was feared but some either lesser or different fear), patients say, "This is easier to manage than the worry." Why? because the future we have created in our minds is devoid of two elements that are given as gifts to us in the present: grace and God's sovereign presence.

God gives grace. He gives not because we deserve it but because he has staked his reputation and person on the perseverance of His saints, "Or do you suppose it is to no purpose that Scripture says 'He yearns jealously over the spirit that he has made to dwell in us,' *But he gives more* grace. Therefore, it says, 'God opposes the proud but gives grace to the humble.' Submit yourselves therefore to God. Resist the devil and he will flee from you" (James 4:5-7, emphasis mine). We are not given grace from God for countless future catastrophic possibilities; we are given grace from God to accomplish that one task he has set before us in this moment.

When, as a child, the Dutch Christian Corrie ten Boom, who helped hide Jewish people from Nazis during the second world war, first saw death, she ran to her father in fear, "I need you. You can't die! You can't," she recounts his response:

> "Father sat down on the edge of the narrow bed. 'Corrie,' he began gently, 'when you and I go to Amsterdam-when do I give you your ticket?' I sniffed a few times, considering this. 'Why, just before we get on the train.' 'Exactly. And our wise Father in heaven knows when we're going to need things, too. Don't run out ahead of Him, Corrie. When the time comes that some of us will have to die, you will look into your heart and find the

strength you need-just in time.'"[88]

And yet, even as we receive God's grace for the moment, our trials and hardships still press in, and we are tempted to fear again. We may hold the ticket to get on the train, but now everything around us seems terribly bad. I return to Corrie ten Boom's advice: "When a train goes through a tunnel and it gets dark, you don't throw away the ticket and jump off. You sit still and trust the engineer."

God's sovereignty is all-encompassing. Nothing is outside his control. As R.C. Sproul proclaimed, "If there is one single molecule in this universe running around loose, totally free of God's sovereignty, then we have no guarantee that a single promise of God will ever be fulfilled."[89] The mind is a powerful tool, a gift, under God's sovereignty, yet it can create hyper-realistic false worlds, worlds that never existed and will never exist. These false realities include vivid pictures, sounds, and smells that can feel as though they are completely real. Yet, these false worlds are missing the one element required to bring them into existence: God's sovereign presence.[90] It is through him that everything created derives its existence. To use an incomplete metaphor, our anxious futures are like making lightbulbs in a world without electricity. Turning the glass in our hands, we feel it as solid and tangible, and it has all the elements of an object capable of producing incandescent light. Yet of what purpose is that glass or metal wire? Of what purpose was the mental time spent designing and crafting this object that ultimately has no purpose?

The future beckons us. It calls for our attention and focus more powerfully than many other distractions.

Effective in the Present

What we have been discussing, living in the past or future, can be best summarized by the Catholic priest Henri Nouwen: "We seem to have a fear of empty spaces. The philosopher Spinoza called this a *horror vacui*. We want to fill up what is empty. Our lives stay very full. And when we are not blinded by busyness, we fill our inner space with guilt about things of the past or worries about things to come."[91] The present is a vacuum waiting to be filled with endless possibilities. When we finally slow our minds to the present, free of past regret and future anxiety, what we are left with is something that threatens to be more fearful than the past or future: the duty of the present. Indeed, while pasts can never be undone and futures may never come, the present is sure, guaranteed, and it will wait for our action only as long as it takes for this present moment to be replaced by the next. The former is forever established, and the latter is filled with a necessity of choice between action and inaction.

In practice, we are prone to filling this duty with one of two errors. They exist like gullies on either side of an effective narrow path: apathy to the present and purposeless busyness.

Apathy. I don't believe anyone is born apathetic. Babies are born grasping for what they need: comfort, warmth, and food. Apathy, it follows, is a consequence of something. Repeated failure often develops into a sense of futility that leads to apathy. Studies in behavioral psychology have shown that behaviors rapidly diminish when they no longer produce a rewarding stimulus. Rats will press levers that deliver food a surprising number of times without tiring, but the food *must* come for them to continue. Eventually, with no food reinforcement, the lever presses stop.

Whether it be working on a marriage, the fight for justice, the eradication of a deadly disease, or keeping a clean home without evidence of progress, we inevitably tire and grow apathetic. This presents a unique challenge in a world that, for Christians, regularly opposes our mission. Though many areas of the world continue to see conversions and revival, other Christians languish in areas, rapidly losing ground. Hopelessness and burnout can quickly follow. It is to this apathy that Psalm 46 speaks. Its instruction to "Be still" may seem like an odd recommendation to the apathetic heart. We often point to inactivity as the telltale sign of apathy, and indeed it is, but it is a symptom, not the cause. The instruction to those experiencing burnout is not to *just do something*. Neither is it "just take a vacation." We must address apathy at its source: the futility and hopelessness that fuels it.

The command to be still in Psalm 46 recalls language from Exodus, where the Israelites were before the Red Sea. For those who have not seen this body of water, it can appear in their mind as a shallow river or, if deep, at least not very wide. This is certainly not the case. The Red Sea was as daunting to the Israelites as the approaching armies of Pharaoh. Caught between two massive adversaries, they became apathetic, "Is it because there are no graves in Egypt that you have taken us away to die in the wilderness?" (Ex. 14:11). The command God provides in Exodus 14:14 to fear not and "stand firm" should feel similar to the command to "be still."

The command to be still or stand firm is not a call to inaction. Shortly after God issued this command, the Israelites must walk faithfully forward across the sea to the other side. We must be careful to avoid the pitfall of inaction under the guise of "being still." This command has more to do with the orientation of our mind and heart than what we do with our hands or feet.

Christians must reorient their hearts towards this Psalm's reasoning for being still, "know that I am God." The one who rests on the throne is not falling behind, losing ground, or retreating. He proclaims His victory "I will be exalted among the nations, I will be exalted in the earth!" (Ps. 46:10b). In Exodus hear God proclaim, "I will get glory over Pharaoh and all his host, his chariots and his horseman. And the Egyptians shall know that I am the LORD" (14:17). It is because of God's sovereignty and ultimate victory that we can continue toiling in places our work seems fruitless.

The Psalm points us to the ultimate victory of the New Jerusalem, "There is a river whose streams make glad the city of God, the holy habitation of the Most High" (v4). This is not a future river from which we will someday drink; it is one we have access to now, and it quenches the thirst of the apathetic heart.

When the present calls for action and our previous attempts have seemed fruitless, and we desire to give up, we can look to our conquering King and act with a stillness only He can provide.

Busyness. The gully of purposeless busyness is on the other side of our road to effectiveness in the present. Busyness is insidious. Rarely do we set out to be busy; instead, busyness results when our brains move tasks to "autopilot." We may continue to do something for months or years without ever reevaluating why we began doing it in the first place. Action out of inertia (i.e., doing something because it's what has been done in the past) is a recipe for ineffectiveness.

Busyness is similarly dangerous because it gives the illusion of being effective. We feel accomplished when we can point to a long to-do list with completed items. The problem is that items off a checklist are of no value if they are working toward the wrong goal or do not have a goal in mind at all.

We may see similarities in this experience to the stories we read of the state of the Temple and its tasks during Jesus' Day. Jesus condemned the Pharisees and scribes, saying, "…for the sake of your tradition you have made void the word of God" (Matt. 15:6b). What God had ordained in his covenant and the work of the Temple was meant to be an outflowing of a heart condition, one of fear and reverence for God. Jesus quotes from Isaiah, "This people honors me with their lips, but their heart is far from me" (Matt. 15:8).

The antidote to busyness is recalling the purpose behind our work. Just as in treating apathy, we must remember God's victory, in busyness, we must recall our purpose in work.

Christians are called to work. Work feels good because we're made for it. God placed Adam and Eve into the Garden of Eden with a job to do; stated another way, work was present before the Fall. Our brains are wired to find purposed work rewarding and supply "feel-good" neurotransmitters like dopamine when we complete a job. This is why busyness can become addictive. The Christian, however, is not called to indiscriminate work but work for a purpose, and this purpose we understand as being for the glory of God (more on this in Chapter 6).

In 2 Peter, we are given instructions for how to avoid becoming "ineffective or unfruitful":

> "For this very reason, make every effort to supplement your faith with virtue, and virtue with knowledge, and knowledge with self-control, and self-control with steadfastness, and steadfastness with godliness, and godliness with brotherly affection, and brotherly affection with love. For if these qualities are yours and are increasing, they keep you from being ineffective or unfruitful in the knowledge of our Lord Jesus Christ." (2 Pet. 1:5-8)

Our effectiveness is rooted in faith, virtue, knowledge, self-control, steadfastness, godliness, brotherly affection, and love because these (though not exhaustively) glorify God. This echoes Jesus' words to "Go and learn what this means: 'I desire mercy, and not sacrifice'" (Matt. 9:13). God is glorified in what we do because there is a heart condition, one of virtue ending in love for Him and others, as its source.

Presence

Effectiveness in the present has been defined mostly in the negative: avoiding the gullies of apathy and purposeless busyness, but it is also to be defined in the positive. As alluded to in the introduction to this chapter, effectiveness in the present is fixing our eyes on a future reality that is somehow, wonderfully, spiritually present right now: that the Kingdom has been inaugurated, that Christ sits at the right hand of the Father, and that he has given us victory over sin and death. When we stop focusing on the past or future, what we are instructed to fix our eyes on is the inaugurated Kingdom, which is soon to be consummated. We do not fix our eyes on what is seen "but to the things that are unseen. For the things that are seen are transient, but the things that are unseen are eternal" (2 Cor. 4:18); this is faith.

Faith is not a hope in a future reality that may or may not occur. Faith is a firm conviction that what has been promised is so sure that though it is unseen now, it is as real as if it were seen.

This is why it is said we walk by faith, not by sight (2 Cor. 5:7) and it is counted to us as blessing, "blessed are those who have not seen and yet believe" (John 20:29). This is the difference between worry and faith. Worry provides us with many scary scenarios that may or may not come true, and we anxiously anticipate how we will respond. Faith points us to a reality that will *assuredly* come true and rests (as we discussed as a treatment for apathy) in our Savior's victory. This is why we can be joyful in trials and tribulations, why we can call them light and momentary (2 Cor. 4:17-18). Without our sure conviction, we have every reason to worry because our light and momentary afflictions instead represent enduring, potentially unending suffering. What my patients report the most distress over is not their current pain but the thought that it might *continue endlessly*. This is not the destiny of Christians.[92] For we have been promised that "He will wipe away every tear from [our] eyes, and death shall be no more, neither shall there be mourning, nor crying, nor pain anymore, for the former things have passed away" (Rev. 21:4). What has passed away were those same things that were formerly *seen*. What has been revealed (*the* Revelation) is what was true all along: that Jesus stands victorious, that sin and death have lost their sting, and that Satan has failed at conquering the Bride of Christ.

Peter exhorts his readers who are facing persecution from false profits and blasphemers by pointing them to what is to come, saying, "The Lord is not slow to fulfill his promise to you..." (2 Pet. 3: 9a). He reminds them that the new heavens and new earth will come in an instant:

> "But the day of the Lord will come like a thief, and then the heavens will pass away with a roar, and the heavenly bodies will be burned up and dissolved, and the earth and the works that are done on it will be exposed...but according to his promise we are waiting for new heavens and a new earth in which righteousness dwells" (2 Pet. 3:10,13).

So what matters is not the circumstances Christians find

themselves in, whether painful or pleasant, in temptation or trial, nor the past or future which our minds so often dwell in, but the sure confidence (faith) that what God has promised is real. This is effective presence.

So what if I lack faith? I hear the question so often in practice I'm tempted to put my response on a business card: you do. I do, too. We should be driven to ask God for more continually. The disciples were in the boat with Jesus on the Sea of Galilee, in the presence of God himself, and they lacked faith. In another instance, Peter has faith enough to get out of the boat but not sustain him in the waves. A young boy's father approaching Jesus for healing cries out, "I believe; help my unbelief!" (Mark 9:24b). This is our cry as well. The heart of God toward those who lack faith but desire to be effective in the present for his kingdom is one of Love and Mercy.

Medicine and Effective Service

Some time ago, I was asked to speak to a community of men who gathered regularly to mutually encourage one another in their fight against pornography and sexual sin. Specifically, I was asked to talk about the ways medication may play a role in their recovery. If you pause for a moment, what is your initial reaction to the use of medication in a struggle against sin?

Perhaps hope rises as you consider those in your own life who have been impacted by addiction of various kinds, or you are aware of the large number of Christians who struggle with pornography, alcohol, opioids, nicotine, and other substances and have wondered if there are medications given in common grace to help in the fight.

Maybe it doesn't sit well with you. Is there something about using a pill to combat a sin struggle that feels like a shortcut or a cop-out? Perhaps a pill might seem like a good idea in the short term, but in the long term, it couldn't possibly be helpful for something so deeply rooted in the fallen nature of the human heart.

I may be projecting my thoughts onto you because I've had both of these run through my head, especially as I prepared to discuss the topic with this group of men. What I wanted to make clear to them, and to anyone who considers medication on their path of sanctification, is that a pill doesn't do the heart work, but it can help as one pursues that work.

Currently, outside the window of my 6th-story apartment, I can see a man smoking. I know very little about him. I can see his uniform, which appears to be of a cook or chef; he looks fatigued by his posture and has squatted down several times, nearly sitting on the pavement outside. I can see the billowing puffs of white/grey smoke that emanate from his face and dissipate in the air above his head. I also know what is happening inside his brain, which neurotransmitters are released, which receptors are filled, and which neurons are firing. I also know what damage is being done to his lungs and the risks he is acquiring because of this dangerous habit. What I don't know is how he started smoking, what his home life is like, what he may be processing mentally, or the state of his soul.

If this man came to my clinic, I know I could offer him something to help reduce some of his cravings or to make it less rewarding to smoke. Still, a pill will never help him solve the issues he may be facing in his marriage, the circumstances that caused him to take up smoking in the first place, or fix potential issues at his job. It also can't heal his relationship with God if he doesn't know Him. The most important things about this man remain unaffected by medication.

But if I can help him stop smoking, perhaps he won't develop lung cancer, or maybe he will have more energy, perhaps he will turn to healthier coping skills that lead to long-term changes in his thinking, the way he works through and displays his emotions to others, the way he talks with his wife or the example he is to his children.

A few years ago, a young pastor came to my office with a sudden onset of crippling fear of public speaking. This was a problem for obvious reasons when he was a key member of a pastoral rotation in which he preached every fourth or fifth Sunday to a rather large congregation. Each time he got to the pulpit, he was overwhelmed with a feeling of intense nausea and sweating and feared he would vomit or faint. He wondered if there was anything I could do. I assured him that this wasn't the first time I'd treated something of this nature and would be happy to offer him an as-needed medication for him to take just before preaching. "I don't want to rely on anything for my preaching," he cautioned me. "Except God," I reminded him, "Oh yes, of course," he smiled. I explained that a non-addictive agent used to help blunt the fight or flight response for just a few Sundays would help him regain his confidence in preaching, and he likely wouldn't need it much longer. I also talked through how God may be using this experience to remind him that without Him and the common graces he provides in medicine, he may be prone to become conceited, believing himself to be the source of strength and power behind the message rather than the Holy Spirit. I also quoted him from AW Tozer, "It is doubtful whether God can bless a man greatly until He has hurt him deeply." God puts His great gospel message in "jars of clay" so that we don't forget from whom the power comes (2 Cor. 4:7-9).

If I remember correctly, he didn't need the medication more than twice before he was back at the podium preaching God's word, and the medication sat unused in some bathroom cabinet until he threw it away. Praise God that even when the medicine sat in the trash, he didn't throw away the memory of God humbling him and graciously providing a tool to assist him in his healing.[93]

We don't take medications, and I don't prescribe them, so we can live an easy, carefree life, but so that we can become more effective in our work and service for the Kingdom. The harvest is too plentiful to allow God's people to lay in bed weak with the physical impact of depression, shaking with anxiety, fatigued due to insomnia, or bound to an addiction. We proclaim God as good in our sickness as in the means of our healing and steward those resources to his ultimate glory through effective work for the Kingdom.

Logotherapy and the Will to Glorify

I hope the implication of this effectivity in the present on human psychology is apparent, namely, that we can work in fields with apparently no progress with hope (avoiding apathy), we can work diligently and not just busily (purposeless busyness), and we can work without fear because of the faith we have in what is promised and as sure as the things that are seen (avoiding anxiety).

What unites all these aspects of effectiveness in the present is the presence of *purposeful work*. Many of my patients are shocked to have their "sitting on clouds" view of heaven replaced with the more accurate "tilling the ground" picture of Eden. Work was present before the fall and will be in the new heavens and earth.

We were made to work. This is evident in our psychology. At key points in the lives of humans, an existential vacuum of meaningful work exists and can lead to anxiety, depression, and insomnia, among other mental health troubles. The parent who, for the first time, finds themselves with an empty nest. The college graduate who finds themselves in the space between walking the stage to get a degree and finding a job. The man who retires after decades of work and finds the golf course doesn't fill that empty space. The elderly Florida couple who searches for one more seashell to complete their collection.[94] The patient who goes on long-term full disability and no longer can work.

The solution isn't to just *do something*, as many find themselves with the same existential vacuum in their jobs. Work was never made to fill that space of meaning and purpose directly. Logotherapy, a psychotherapeutic technique invented by Dr. Viktor Frankl, focuses on a person's "Will to Meaning" and the psychological malady that results when this primary drive remains unfulfilled. He outlines three values in which humans may find fulfillment of this Will to Meaning: creative values, experiential values, and attitudinal values.

Frankl's values have a solid footing in human life. We find fulfillment in creative acts and experiences, and when neither of those is within our control (such as in forced suffering), in our chosen attitude in response to the circumstance.

In the modified theory I propose, these values, if not rooted in what we may term the "Will to Glorify God," ultimately fall short of creating ultimate purpose and meaning.

Take the example of suffering, far and above selecting our attitude towards suffering which provides some level of comfort, a suffering which is purposed for the glory of God provides fulfillment that lasts, "Therefore let those who suffer according to God's will entrust their souls to a faithful Creator *while doing good*" (1 Pet. 4:19, emphasis mine). This is not good for its own sake but good to the glory of God.

We see the impact of a Will to Glorify God in the wealthy financiers who achieved their fortunes by dishonest means, spending their time and energies in work that was corrupt and far from glorifying God. They may look content, but inwardly, they feel empty. Alternatively, we have the penniless relief worker who sleeps next to those they serve in a third-world country and rests content knowing the gospel has been preached, and God was glorified in it.

Perhaps we find ourselves doing something mundane and are tempted to view our work as worthless or at least not as meaningful as some "greater" or "higher" calling: emptying the dishwasher, changing a diaper, and changing the car's oil. Instead, we may feel that we should be on the street corner preaching, writing books, lecturing to packed auditoriums, teaching life lessons to children, or any other number of tasks we have identified as more important. The Will to Glorify God identifies that whatever task God has called us to in this present moment is what we should be doing, and to His glory.

We are not born with this Will to Glorify God. We are born with its competing partner, the Will to Glorify Self. This painful truth led to the Fall: we desired to glorify ourselves rather than our Creator. The disorganization of the world began first in the human mind and heart, flowed out into disordered behavior (doing what God told us not to do), and subsequently disordered the entire world of created things, which longs for its reordering in the New Creation (Rom. 8:22). It is a work of the Holy Spirit, not of ourselves, that transforms a Will to Glorify Self into the Will to Glorify God. We wrestle with these competing wills our entire lives, desiring to be "deliver[ed] from this body of death" (Rom. 7:24) and made new.

To look at how these two Wills interact with our model of Integrated Christian Psychiatry (Figure 3), we see that the Will to Glorify Self, as warned of in scripture and our lived experiences as Christians, can lead to problems. As stated earlier, this does not mean that all problems come from personal sin. Still, the stain of original sin, rooted in the Will to Glorify Self, certainly explains the presence of suffering in the world.

The good gifts of modern medicine, as many have pointed out, risk feeding back into our Will to Glorify Self if not stewarded correctly. This is especially a risk for non-Christians who do not have a Will to Glorify God, but it can also be a pitfall for Christians as they utilize gifts of common grace. The Will to Glorify God encourages and strengthens our pursuit after increased knowledge of God, conformity into the likeness of Christ, and effectiveness for the Kingdom.

We are made to work, that is clear, but more specifically, we are made to work for the glory of God. Until the Will to Glorify God is realized, incompletely now and completely in heaven, we are bound to feel an existential dread. For now, when Christ died, he did so to "redeem us from all lawlessness and to purify for himself a people for his own possession who are zealous for good works" (Titus 2:14) that we might glorify God in that work.

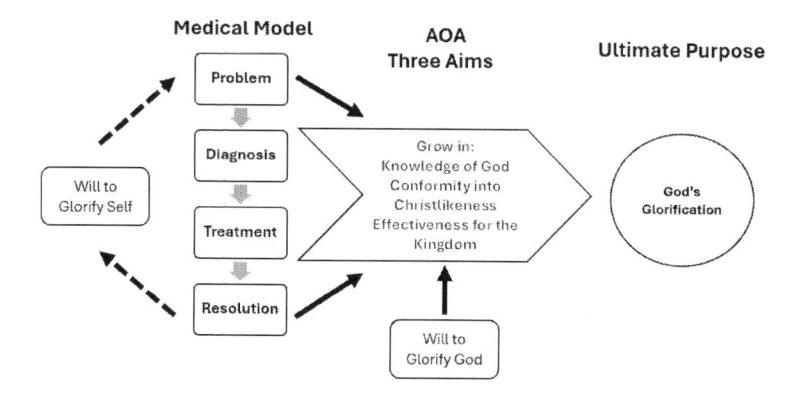

Figure 3. Integrating the Will to Glorify Self and the Will to Glorify God into the proposed model of Integrated Christian Psychiatry.

Adam O'Neill

CHAPTER 6

...TO THE GLORY OF GOD.

"The greater our present trials, the louder will our future songs be."
CHARLES SPURGEON

Made to Glorify God

Reading this book, some may say, at times, my tone is melancholy. The themes we discuss in this book are heavy, from the fall of mankind, to psychiatric and physical illness, conflicts in the body of Christ, and misused good gifts. We've discussed these things because they take place in the lives of believers. For, as those who have followed the Lord for any portion of time find, it is not an easy path on which he takes us. A patient recently lamented, "But the non-Christians seem so happy." Many of them are, and we could wish that they weren't for their own sake. For the unredeemed, this is the only pleasure or happiness they will experience for the rest of eternity. For Christians, our loving savior bids us come with Him carrying our cross so that we may die. With the weight of a cursed tree on our back, we shudder at the uphill climb ahead. This is the narrow way. I wanted to make that terrible truth evident in this book because many who pick it up will be in that place. Perhaps a faithful Christian going through the dark night of the soul asking *why* a good God would allow this in their lives? A provider who acutely sees the fall's impact on her patients and becomes weary precisely because she loves them and so hates the sin and sickness that plague them. Heaven forbid I proclaim a happy theology to them. How trite it will all feel. How unworthy of suffering does happiness feel when we actually experience it?

But to my fellow weary traveler, we press on because we see the glory ahead, only in glimpses and only for a moment. We see our Savior's radiant face, though dimly, and sense this is the answer to all the pain and suffering. Not *happiness* but *Him*.

Along the way, He has given good gifts, principally in this book, we have discussed those in holistic psychiatry; recall that at the beginning of this book, I described the process of pursuing mental wellness like preparing an archer to fire an arrow at a target. The common grace good of science and medicine are much like the preparation of a finely crafted bow or the alignment of the feathers, the sharpness of the arrowhead, and the tautness of the string. So, too, the gifts of psychology in understanding the mind, like training the archer, building his strength, steadying his hand, and calming his breathing. Science, medicine, and psychology are noble callings, yet I have argued that it was ultimately useless if we aligned that archer opposite its target.

The world would point to many potential targets: freedom from pain, success at work, financial gain, inner peace, and happiness. None of these is worthy of being our ultimate goal.

St. Augustine writes in *The Confessions*, "All men are united by one purpose, temporal happiness on earth, and all that they do is aimed at this goal, although in the endless variety of their struggles to attain it, they pitch and toss like waves of the sea." What a succinct definition of the Will to Glorify Self.

Only the glorification of God is a sufficient target for our efforts in mental health, indeed for our lives as a whole. Relief of pain, financial gain, and happiness are not necessarily wrong. Indeed, they do occasionally exist along the believer's path, but if they are the ultimate goal, what we find instead is that we either miss them entirely and feel we have failed or achieve them (perhaps worse) and find they could not satisfy.

The gifts of modern medicine and psychology are tools; they assist us in what I describe to my patients as the "Three Aims," which we have discussed in the preceding chapters: to increase in knowledge of God, to be conformed into the likeness of His Son, and to become more effective for the kingdom. However, in the end, they are revealed to be just one aim accomplished through a non-linear, ever-developing path of sanctification to God's glory. As we come to know God better, we see how he has ordered the world and how it has been impacted by the Fall; we also see his awesome sovereignty and goodness not despite nor in the absence of, but in and through, suffering, in His working all things for the good of His elect. As we come to know God better, we see how we reflect Him and how His holiness reveals our fallenness; we are driven, not out of fear but out of love, to be conformed more into the likeness of our Savior. As we look progressively more like Jesus, we begin to see the world and its brokenness and how our giftedness and equipping have made us more effective in advancing the gospel. In each of these steps, we glorify God. This is authentic psychology; this is rightly oriented personhood.

I hope many patients read this book, but briefly, it is to my colleagues in the healing arts that I now speak directly. To you, by training and accreditation, you have been given the script pad, the counseling office, and the status of serving as a healer—this is a weighty burden. It is good that non-Christians may occasionally find themselves in the care of a Christian provider like yourself, for in binding their wounds, they catch a glimpse of the hands and feet of Jesus. We do a good and noble thing by identifying cognitive distortions, correcting faulty thinking patterns, and encouraging better behaviors and healthier relationships. But remember, any good gifts of medicine or psychology separated from the pursuit of our savior become pleasant distractions.[95] Beware lest your patients look too closely at the bandages, gauze, and pills and miss what is infinitely greater still. Greater than the instruments of healing (of which you are included) is the Healer. We do not deny that medicine is good; we point to the one who gave it and proclaim Him as greater. You, my Christian colleague, glorify God in your healing arts. This is both a statement of fact and an exhortation.

It is our ultimate end as patients and providers, on earth now and in heaven then, to glorify God. Now, we reflect only dimly as the moon reflects the sun's light. But one day, both in our substance and reflection, we will reflect the glory of our Creator God, and sin, which will be no more, and the knowledge of redemption, which will be the last and only remaining echo of sin's former presence will serve to magnify the difference between what was wrong and what is now wholly sanctified forever.[96]

Soli Deo Gloria and Dying to Self

A patient once sat in my office, particularly distressed by a peculiar verse of the Bible. The verse itself was not peculiar; rather, it was peculiar because it isn't one I encounter frequently causing distress. Under an English Standard Version heading of John's gospel "The Purpose of This Book," we read, "but these are written so that you may believe that Jesus is the Christ, the Son of God, and that by believing you may have life in his name" (John 20:30b). "What does it mean to have life?" my patient asked, his concern now becoming clearer. My patient wondered how we might identify this life to know if we have it. The implied doubt was that he, in fact, did not possess it. "What image do you have when you think of this life John speaks about?" I asked. He described a type of friend he had encountered many times who seemed to be "high on life," infrequently if ever weary, and assured of their standing in Christ, "I don't know if I've had that and if I have, certainly not frequently."

Life in Christ carries a similar connotation in many of my patients' lives. It's been an image I've held in my mind as well, but I want to suggest that "Life," as we may define it as Christians, is less about our felt experience (emotional, psychological, physical) and more about Jesus. Its evidence in our lives is what it drives us to do: self-sacrifice, boldness, and future hope for the glory of God.

Turning to Paul as he addresses the Corinthians:

> "We are afflicted in every way, but not crushed; perplexed, but not driven to despair; persecuted, but not forsaken; struck down, but not destroyed; always carrying in the body the death of Jesus, so that the life of Jesus may also be manifested in our bodies. For we who live are always being given over to death for Jesus' sake, so that the life of Jesus may also be manifested

in our mortal flesh. So death is at work in us, but life in you. Since we have the same spirit of faith according to what has been written, 'I believed, and so I spoke, we also believe, and so we also speak, knowing that he who raised the Lord Jesus will raise us also with Jesus and bring us with you into his presence. For it is all for your sake, so that as grace extends to more and more people it may increase in thanksgiving, to the glory of God" (2 Cor. 4:8-18).

Afflicted, perplexed, persecuted, struck down, carrying in the body the death of Jesus, this is life? Indeed, "For if we have been united with him in a death like his, we shall certainly be united with him in a resurrection like his" (Rom. 6:5). Life comes through the death of self and new life to Christ to the glory of God. This is why we are led to self-sacrifice: "So death is at work in us, but life in you" (2 Cor. 4:12). To boldness: "So that as grace extends to more and more people it may increase in thanksgiving, to the glory of God (v15b). To a future hope: "as we look not to the things that are seen but to the things that are unseen. For the things that are seen are transient, but the things that are unseen are eternal" (v18).

The life we live is no longer ours "but Christ who lives in me" (Gal. 2:20). If it is now Christ's life we live, his mission will be our mission, his path our path, and his end our end. His mission was and is to glorify the Father, his path filled with hardship, pain, and suffering, and his end: that of glorification, dominion, and power he has made to be our end as well. Praise be to God!

The lie many Christians, especially those in the West, have come to believe is that life in Christ has principally more to do with a person's prosperity and pleasure. Jesus' words, "I came that they may have life and have it abundantly," in John 10, become, in the wrong hands, evidence of God's ultimate desire for your earthly success and happiness. We begin to feel as though we are missing something when our Christian walk instead looks more like Paul's: afflicted, perplexed, persecuted... Yet, this is life. And so he writes, "and he died for all, that those who live might no longer live for themselves but for him who for their sake died and was raised" (2 Cor. 5:15).

The Reformation anthem Soli Deo Gloria (for the glory of God alone) points to what must occur (God's glorification) and what that process requires: a death to self and a new life in Christ. This profound truth has far-reaching implications for our mental health.

When we die to ourselves, we are left only with the rightly oriented thought: *it's all about Him.* We step down off the throne of our hearts, stop viewing every world event, unkind or kind gesture, blessing or curse as chapters in a story in which we are the main character and instead see our lives, our friends and family, our communities and world as players in a cosmic drama to the glory of God. So what happens practically with this shift in perspective?

Our eyes are turned away from earthly promises and pleasures to our true source of hope. These temporary good gifts are included in the "transient things" Paul describes in verse 18. Good gifts of God must remain good gifts because when the weight of a soul rests on them, they collapse beneath the weight. We may be tempted to view good gifts as inherently bad rather than bad due to their proportion. Many of the most joyful blessings can easily become the most dangerous idols. We see this when relationships become ultimate sources of identity and joy, children's successes say more about us than is healthy, and our work crowds out family, service to the

Church, or worship. When cars don't just get us from point A to B safely but serve as status symbols for how far we've made it in life. Good gifts turn into roadblocks in our race of Faith.

When our perspective changes our eyes and hearts are transfixed on the eternal things that last. We see the world differently. We have progressively more peace in hardship as we recognize the time limit set on our suffering; we appreciate but do not anxiously acquire material wealth or possessions; our relationships become ways to joyfully serve rather than selfishly attempting to meet all our needs. In light of eternal things, the temporal things seem incomparably smaller.[97]

Our hardships are seen not as punishments from God but as a divine blueprint for our sanctification to His glory. There is an unbearable weight of condemnation many of my patients feel regarding their mental health struggles. In the deep grooves of a sculptor's chisel, they instead feel a crushing blow from the divine gavel of justice. This pain is unbearable because we weren't meant to carry it. This pain was experienced instead in our place, on the cross. It was the dark night our Savior endured so that on our divine ledger, in place of our debt, "paid in full" could be written instead. Yes, suffering can result from our sin, but the heart of our God is inclined toward us in those moments, not away. Thomas Goodwin writes,

> "The greater the misery is, the more is the pity when the party is beloved. Now of all miseries, sin is the greatest; and while you look at it as such, Christ will look upon it a such also. And he, loving your persons, and hating only the sin, his hatred shall all fall, and that only upon the sin, to free you of it by its ruin and destruction, but his affections shall be the more drawn out to you; and this as much when you lie under sin as under any other affliction. Therefore fear not."[98]

Paul's description of the Christian walk may be characterized by affliction, persecution, and death to self, but what it produces for us is far greater: a rightly oriented view of God's temporal good gifts, the promise of our unseen future glory, and the promise that all things, sufferings not just included but especially, are working for the good of the elect and for God's glory.

Glory as Currency of Heaven

The preceding section focused heavily on Paul's letter to the Corinthians and the fourth chapter, which describes the life and light of the gospel. It leads Paul and his fellow believers to self-sacrifice, boldness, and hope for the future, but what is this hope for the future? "For this light and momentary affliction is preparing for us an eternal weight of glory beyond all comparison, as we look not to the things that are seen but to the things that are unseen. For the things that are seen are transient, but the things that are unseen are eternal" (2 Cor. 4:17-18). It may be helpful to imagine what glory would look like in heaven, but first, we must see what it looks like on earth.

A strange trend emerged online in early 2023 where women asked the men in their lives, "How often do you think about the Roman Empire?" and recorded their candid responses to post. I discovered this trend one Sunday afternoon when my sister called to ask me that very question. The question caught me off guard, but I thought carefully, remembering that that very morning, as I walked to church, I passed by the towering dome of the Capital of the United States and saw the massive columns of stone that make up the impressive structure, I thought about its architectural origins and how it resembled images I have seen from ancient Rome. I answered, "Oddly enough, this morning, but I would imagine usually once a week," to which she burst into laughter, "I never think about the Roman Empire; why do men think about it so much?".

I called a good friend to make sure I wasn't alone. He reassured me, "I think it's because of the gladiators, the government structure, and their various inventions that have persisted through time; you can't escape them, and men's brains think like that." Gladiators, government, ingenuity, it all screamed of glory. So, too, this sparkling "City on a Hill" we call Washington, D.C.

Earthly glory is built upon the strong conquering the weak, acquiring and sustaining power by any means necessary, and accumulating exorbitant wealth, among other sordid pursuits. We don't need to look to antiquity for this definition of glory. From high-impact contact sports to corporate ladders, power is pursued, and "the winner takes all."

Our radical gospel points us to a suffering servant King who bids his followers to come and die to see that "the last will be first, and the first last" (Matt. 20:16). His disciples would naturally follow this path. From Stephen, the first martyr, to today, Christians have been called to give up their life as Jesus did. But though they died by stoning, burning, hanging, crucifying, and starvation, among many other tortures, we should not see weakness. Here, in the precious death of His saints (Ps. 116:15), is a different kind of glory.

Stephen was given a glimpse of these unseen things as the crowd hurled stones at him until he died. His words must have stuck with Saul, who oversaw his execution: "But he, full of the Holy Spirit, gazed into heaven and saw the glory of God, and Jesus was standing at the right hand of God. And he said, 'Behold, I see the heavens opened, and the Son of Man standing at the right hand of God'" (Acts 7:56). What appeared as earthly weakness, passivism, or surrender was a heavenly kind of glory which outshines and undoes our earthly conception of glory.

I submit that glory is the currency of heaven. It is the reflected Shekhinah glory of God seen in the radiant faces of his Saints. Not all have been called to give up their lives for the sake of the gospel; the ones who have have a high calling, but all are called to take up their crosses and follow after the Savior on the *Via Dolorosa*. This is the "weight of glory beyond all comparison" produced by the "light and momentary trials" Paul discusses in 2 Corinthians 4:17.

When we recognize what suffering is doing for us, we can proclaim, as Charles Spurgeon did: "Glory be to God for the furnace, the hammer, and the file. Heaven shall be all the fuller of bliss because we have been filled with anguish here below, and earth shall be better tilled because of our training in the school of adversity."

Currency has value because it has a source. In the United States, printed money carries weight, originally because precious metals backed it and today because it is backed by the "Full faith and credit of the United States of America." Our unseen and eternal glory likewise has a backing. The shed blood of God purchased it, a value much higher than precious metals or governmental support.

Our "glory-currency" also has a source. It is meant to be cast to Jesus. He is the securer, issuer, source, and destiny of all glory, honor, and power (Ps. 24:10, Ps. 115:1, John 17:24, Phil. 4:20, Rom. 11:36, Rev. 4:11).

Words of the recently composed Hymn, "All Glory Be to Christ," encapsulate well the relationship between earthly efforts and heavenly glory,

> "Should nothing of our efforts stand, no legacy survive, unless the Lord does raise the house, in vain its builders strive. To you who boast tomorrow's gain, tell me, what is your life? A mist, it vanishes at dawn, all glory be to Christ."[99]

Ironically, a rightly oriented psychology—the study of self—has little to do with us and much to do with God, for as we have stated, it is "in him that we live and move and have our being" (Acts 17:28).

Though the Bible gives relatively little information on what heaven will exactly be like, I imagine one of the ways we will spend eternity is by telling the stories of how God has been faithful in and through our earthly trials. Like angled mirrors, we reflect God's glory to one another through the narrative of our earthly lives. Perhaps this is part of what it is like not to need a sun because He is our light (Rev. 21:23). His brilliant glory emanates, reflecting off of us and to one another so that we shine brighter than any temporal sun.

Made to See God's Glory

There's something about this brilliant and emanating glory that we long to see. Not only were we made to glorify God, we were made to *see* His glory.

There are moments when seeing something leaves you speechless: standing before the Grand Canyon, seeing the sun descend below the horizon across the ocean, seeing your bride appear while you wait for her at the altar, or experiencing the miracle of childbirth. It's as if a missing piece of our human experience has been found, and we may wonder how this intangible sense could feel so tangible. Vision is indeed unique.

For centuries, the philosophical problem was proposed: could someone who was born blind and was able to feel shapes (i.e., blocks, spheres, etc.) be able to identify those objects by sight alone if they regain their sight? This thought problem was unsolvable for a long time because medical technology could not restore sight. But, in 2003, it became possible. When the experiment was trialed, the person born blind could not differentiate objects they had long since felt while blind. It's as if the object they had felt and "known" was utterly new to them.[100] Touch helped them know in a way, but sight helped them know more fully. What about in the reverse?

Take a moment to look around you and imagine what something you can see feels like. My guess is that you can fairly accurately guess what something feels like by sight. Sight is foundational; from it, we build our understanding of the structure, function, and nature of things. For this reason, sight has been used to represent knowledge and truth allegorically.

The Pharisees, in their lie (to be without sin), are blind (John 9:40-41), and the disciples are blinded with logs in their eyes, picking specs out of others (Matt. 7:3-4). Faith (confidence in things not seen) (2 Cor. 5:7) becomes sight in its consummation as we see Him as He is (1 John 3:2).

You were made to see God. You were made to walk with him as Adam and Eve did. The Fall has blinded us. We cannot see him as we were created to because sin has obscured our vision. Yet we long, nonetheless.

Take the progression of Moses. In Exodus, he hid his face from the burning bush "for he was afraid to look at God" (Ex. 3:6). Then, later, he asked God on the mountain that he might see him (Ex. 33), and in Exodus 34 descends from the mountain after conversing with God with his face shining with God's glory. The more closely Moses came to *know* God, the more Moses wanted to *see* God. He who heard his voice from the midst of the burning bush (Deut. 4:12) longed to see Him face to face.

We long to see him, but in our sinful state, his radiant face causes us fear. Take, for example, Elijah. To encourage Elijah, God manifested himself, and in response to God's presence, Elijah pulled his cloak over his face.

"Show us the Father," the disciples asked (John 14:8). Yet when Peter, James, and John saw Jesus in his glorified state in the Transfiguration, they were terrified. Peter fell to the ground. We are reminded of Isaiah's presence before the throne. The glory of God causes him to fear he would perish, "And I said: 'Woe is me! For I am lost; for I am a man of unclean lips, and I dwell in the midst of a people of unclean lips; for my eyes have seen the King, the Lord of hosts!'" (Isa. 6:5).

God has ordained that we should see him. How? In holiness, we may see God; we read, "Blessed are the pure in heart, for they shall see God" (Matt. 5:8).

Moses and Elijah, those who while on earth longed and asked to see God, were in the transfiguration not hiding in a rock, seeing only His backside, not in a still small voice or a burning bush, but conversing, surrounded by the glory radiant from the face of Jesus. Not only were you made to glorify God, but in your glorification of Him, He has made you to see Him, "For now we see in a mirror dimly, but then face to face. Now I know in part; then I shall know fully, even as I have been fully known" (1 Cor. 13:12).

We were all made to see God, "Behold He is coming with the cloud, and every eye will see Him" (Rev. 1:7). To those washed in the blood of Jesus and made pure "shall behold [His] face in righteousness; [they] will be satisfied with [His] likeness when [they] awake" (Ps. 17:15). To those who rejected him, they will see him in terror, "calling to the mountains and rocks, 'Fall on us and hide us from the face of him who is seated on the throne, and from the wrath of the Lamb, for the great day of their wrath has come, and who can stand?'" (Rev. 6:16-17).

For the unredeemed, this is not a beatific vision but one of terror. For those who are His, seeing Him as we were made to is our ultimate enjoyment.

Made to Glorify God in our Enjoyment of Him

Maybe you have rummaged through old tools at a yard sale or found your grandfather's shed with unknown gardening, fishing, farming, or automotive implements. As a young boy, I'd often held one in my hand and turned it over, uncertain of its use. There seemed to be levers in various places, parts that moved and others that held fast. Some parts felt sturdy, as if they could withstand heavy weight, and others bent or twisted in places with just a gentle push. What a great mystery it all was, and I felt, to be honest, unsettled. Perhaps, like me, you were curious and *needed* to know. This discomfort dissolved when knowingly my father or grandfather noticed my confusion and came over to show me how it worked. Suddenly, it all made sense; the ingenuity and craftsmanship of the inventor came into view, and I could see how this tool (in the proper hands) could make a difficult task much more manageable. Not only did it work, it worked well, and that felt good.

I view ourselves much like these once-foreign tools in my grandfather's shed. Many people are turning elements of their lives over in their hands, wondering how it all fits. Deep down, we know we are made to experience deep and abiding joy, but we aren't sure how the pieces we've been given make acquiring that joy any easier, much less possible. That is, until we discover how it all works. Like a finely designed tool, we were made to experience joy through the enjoyment produced by glorifying God. When we seek joy outside of his glorification, it's like we are holding the wrong end of an antique push mower. We wonder why the sharp ends hurt our hands as we frustratingly push the handle against the grass. It doesn't work.

Jonathan Edwards said, "God's purpose for my life was that I have a passion for God's glory and that I have a passion for my joy in that glory, and that these two are one passion." John Piper states the bi-directionality of this truth, "God is most glorified in us when we are most satisfied in Him." He has made us such that we can experience no more profound joy, peace, hope, or love than when we are glorifying Him, and we most glorify him as we experience these blessings. What a God we serve!

I sincerely hope I have made much of God in this book. One of the most pivotal moments in my Christian walk was the freedom of knowing this grand story we call life didn't have me at the center. I realized, and continue to see, how I had made much of myself and invited God into *my* story rather than vice versa. What followed that realization was not the immediate relief of every pain but rather the growth of an abiding joy rooted in the relentless pursuit of His glorification.

If I've said anything true in this book, if anything has brought glory to Jesus, it is only a shadow of things to come. One day, this book will be gladly tossed at his feet. The truths it has only glimpsed and proclaimed will be replaced by Truth Himself.[101] Permanent and ours to enjoy forever.

What I can't comprehend, and what provides me comfort beyond measure, is what you or I won't have to lay at his feet, not because there is anything we would withhold, but because he holds it already. There, beside the trophies and crowns, are the painful memories, the stories displayed as scars on our bodies, the tears he has collected in his bottle, and the times he recounted our tossing in his book (Ps. 56:8). Each sleepless night, hospital room prayer, every memory of a saints graveside (Ps. 116:15) written on his nail-pierced hands (Isa. 52:4). He will wipe every tear from our eyes and our bodies and minds finally made new and radiating His glory, "for the former things have passed away" (Rev. 21:4).

Until then, I invite you, as you pursue mental health and wellness, with me to confidently orient our hearts and minds in the direction of the words of the doxology. Here, we see a glorious assent to the source and relationship between good gifts and our gift Giver. We see a call to both heaven and earth, material and immaterial, to orient our lives around the glorification of our Creator. Finally, we see the revelation of that great, powerful, mysterious relationship of the three

Persons of the Godhead, a relationship into which we are lovingly invited. I believe the doxology best encapsulates those truths I have tried my hardest to express in the previous chapters and is a fitting way to end.[102] Mental wellness is not the end-all of our pursuit; to know, see, and serve God is. May He be ever glorified in his people as we walk this brief but difficult road until we may live with Him forever. Come quickly, Lord Jesus.

Praise God from whom all blessings flow. Praise Him, all creatures here below. Praise Him above you, heavenly host. Praise Father, Son, and Holy Ghost.

Adam O'Neill

'

ABOUT THE AUTHOR

Adam O'Neill is a Psychiatric Physician Assistant and owner of a practice in the suburbs of Washington, DC. He attended Wheaton College, where he earned his Bachelor of Arts in Psychology and a Master of Science from Thomas Jefferson University in Philadelphia. His other works include *The Mind After Eden: Psychiatry in a Post-Fall World* and *The Patience of Hope: Encouragement for the Sufferer through the Life and Preaching of George Matheson*. He lives in Northern Virginia and is a member of Capitol Hill Baptist Church.

Adam O'Neill

ENDNOTES

[1] In actuality, ECT is an effective therapy that barely resembles what is seen on television and movies.

[2] For the Christian, looking upward to our Creator does not necessitate having all other physical, emotional, and cognitive needs met. In fact, Matthew 4:4 instructs us that it is not "bread alone" or any other physical need through which we find fulfillment and purpose "but by every word that comes from the mouth of God." Indeed, it is often in times of great physical or psychological need that some are led to greater transcendent thoughts about the nature or purpose of the world and suffering.

[3] John Calvin said, "The human heart is a perpetual idol factory", so not only are we primarily worshipers, our inclination is to worship anything *but* God.

Calvin J. *Institutes of the Christian Religion*. Presbyterian Board of Publication and Sabbath-School Work; 1921. Chapter 11.

[4] Augustine S. *The Confessions*. OUP Oxford; 2008.

[5] There are other forms of epistemology. Within the scientific method itself, it is well understood that the absence of evidence is not evidence of absence.

[6] More about the impact of the fall on human psychology in Chapter 2.

[7] Though Docetism claimed Jesus only *appeared* as a physical being, it was condemned as heretical at the First Council of Nicaea in 325. Notably, many heresies exist because of misunderstandings of the nature of Christ and the Incarnation. Since the beginning, we have struggled with understanding the body/soul relationship

[8] Commentary on St. Paul's First Letter to the Corinthians 15: lec. 2. *Commentary on the Letters of Saint Paul to the Corinthians*. Aquinas Institute for the Study of Sacred Doctrine; 2012.

[9] The danger in the integration view, I believe, is that it can be done very poorly, and people will still label it "integration." For example, a provider sees and assesses a patient, crafts a medical regimen, and then prays with the patient at the end of the visit. I believe it's a victory that a patient and clinician prayed together, but that style of integration is no more integrated than oil and water shaken together. Give it a moment, and things will settle out. For this reason, I've called it "Oil and Water Integration". I've heard from others some variation of, "I'm a Christian and I practice secular medicine, but they don't influence one another", as a definition of integration. This style is even more removed from what I propose as a truly integrated practice. Integration is rooted in the knowledge of our created nature as both physical and nonphysical and a belief that all good and true things come from God. In light of these two fundamental truths, the practitioner approaches a patient to apply the good gifts of common grace so that God may be more greatly glorified in their patient's life.

[10] Augustine S. *The Confessions*. OUP Oxford; 2008.

[11] Attributed to St. Francis of Assisi.

[12] It is worth noting that the beauty of the incarnation is that God humbled himself to take on flesh, to step fully into our experience as humans. It is not enough to have *knowledge* of what being a human is like; there must be a lived experience. The law would not be fulfilled by a deity with knowledge of humanity. Likewise, Jesus was not half human and half God. He was *fully* God and *fully* man. He fulfilled the law in his full humanity, yet always remaining fully God.

[13] This makes the ideal psychologist a thoughtful and inquisitive Christian. I also classify ministers as psychologists, affirming that the secular world does not have exclusive rights to this particular domain.

[14] Conners E. Americans Express Worry Over Personal Safety in Annual Anxiety and Mental Health Poll. Psychiatry.org. Accessed July 27, 2024. https://www.psychiatry.org/news-room/news-releases/annual-anxiety-and-mental-health-poll-2023

[15] Kuntz L. A Year of 988: The First Step in a Long Journey. Published online July 10, 2023. Accessed July 27, 2024. https://www.psychiatrictimes.com/view/a-year-of-988-the-first-step-in-a-long-journey

[16] Products - Data Briefs - Number 464 - April 2023. doi:10.15620/cdc:125705

[17] The following titles result from a Barnes & Noble Top Psychology Books search on October 16, 2023.

[18] Freud S. *The Future of an Illusion*. L. & Virginia Woolf at the Hogarth Press and the Institute of psycho-analysis; 1928.

[19] Colasanto M, Madigan S, Korczak DJ. Depression and inflammation among children and adolescents: A meta-analysis. *J Affect Disord*. 2020;277:940-948. doi:10.1016/j.jad.2020.09.025

[20] Ventriglio A, Sancassiani F, Contu MP, et al. Mediterranean Diet and its Benefits on Health and Mental Health: A Literature Review. *Clin Pract Epidemiol Ment Health*. 2020;16(Suppl-1):156-164. doi:10.2174/1745017902016010156

[21] DiNicolantonio JJ, O'Keefe JH, Wilson W. Subclinical magnesium deficiency: a principal driver of cardiovascular disease and a public health crisis. *Open Heart*. 2018;5(1):e000668. doi:10.1136/openhrt-2017-000668

[22] Liao Y, Xie B, Zhang H, et al. Efficacy of omega-3 PUFAs in depression: A meta-analysis. *Transl Psychiatry*. 2019;9(1):190. doi:10.1038/s41398-019-0515-5

[23] Genedi M, Janmaat IE, Haarman B (Benno) CM, Sommer IEC. Dysregulation of the gut–brain axis in schizophrenia and bipolar disorder: probiotic supplementation as a supportive treatment in psychiatric disorders. *Current Opinion in Psychiatry*. 2019;32(3):185-195.

doi:10.1097/YCO.0000000000000499

[24] Grosso G. Nutritional Psychiatry: How Diet Affects Brain through Gut Microbiota. *Nutrients*. 2021;13(4):1282. doi:10.3390/nu13041282

[25] Koppenol E, Terveer EM, Vendrik KEW, et al. Fecal microbiota transplantation is associated with improved aspects of mental health of patients with recurrent *Clostridioides difficile* infections. *Journal of Affective Disorders Reports*. 2022;9:100355. doi:10.1016/j.jadr.2022.100355

[26] Bartova L, Dold M, Volz HP, Seifritz E, Möller HJ, Kasper S. Beneficial effects of Silexan on co-occurring depressive symptoms in patients with subthreshold anxiety and anxiety disorders: randomized, placebo-controlled trials revisited. *Eur Arch Psychiatry Clin Neurosci*. 2023;273(1):51-63. doi:10.1007/s00406-022-01390-z

[27] See O'Neill A. *The Mind after Eden: Psychiatry in a Post-Fall World*. Independently published; 2022. Chapter "On the Use of Psychiatric Medications",

O'Neill A. Antidepressants aren't happy pills. Faith and Medicine Foundation. Accessed July 27, 2024. https://www.faithandmedicine.foundation/resources/antidepressants-arent-happy-pills,

O'Neill A. Should Christians treat ADHD with medication? Faith and Medicine Foundation. Accessed July 27, 2024. https://www.faithandmedicine.foundation/resources/should-christians-treat-adhd-with-medication

[28] Cuijpers P, Sijbrandij M, Koole SL, Andersson G, Beekman AT, Reynolds CF. Adding Psychotherapy to Antidepressant Medication in Depression and Anxiety Disorders: a Meta-Analysis. *FOC*. 2014;12(3):347-358. doi:10.1176/appi.focus.12.3.347

[29] See this discussion with colleagues of mine on their podcast, Counsel for Life:

Faith or Pharmacy? Christians and psychiatric medications, Featuring Adam O'Neill. Listen Notes. Published October 25, 2023. Accessed July 27, 2024. https://www.listennotes.com/bg/podcasts/counsel-for-life/faith-or-pharmacy-christians-uesVxTQ2-Zf/

[30] Browning EB. *Aurora Leigh: A Poem in Nine Books*. T.Y. Crowell; 1883. Book 7.

[31] Spurgeon CH. *Encouragement for the Depressed.* Crossway; 2020.

[32] Coe JH, Hall TW. *Psychology in the Spirit: Contours of a Transformational Psychology.* InterVarsity Press; 2010.

[33] O'Neill A. *The Patience of Hope: Encouragement for the Sufferer through the Life and Preaching of George Matheson.* Adam O'Neill & Associates LLC; 2024. (emphasis his).

[34] See also Chapter 1 on the dual nature of humans.
[35] We are the created, not the Creator. These are God's communicable and incommunicable attributes, and we will explore their relationship to mental health in Chapter 4).
[36] See the Gospel of Mark, Chapter 5.
[37] "O Love, that will not let me go." George Matheson. See also my book on Matheson's life and hymn:

O'Neill A. *The Patience of Hope: Encouragement for the Sufferer through the Life and Preaching of George Matheson.* Adam O'Neill & Associates LLC; 2024.

[38] Frankl VE. *Man's Search for Meaning.* Noura Books; 2018.

[39] As we discussed at length in Chapter 1.
[40] John Piper once said, "These doctrines are not mainly there to entertain our intellects, they are there to provide rocks under our feet when everything around our souls give way, which it will sooner or later in your life." Doctrines of Grace Seminar Lesson 1 (2008)
[41] The debate as to what to call those in the faith who have resisted the tide of Christian liberalism and pursued the doctrine of the reformers has had no shortage of suggested titles. Reformed is, of course, a frontrunner though others have proposed conservative, evangelical, fundamentalist, orthodox, or Calvinist. Each has its strengths and weaknesses. My preference is orthodox but primarily based on etymology (meaning right teaching). I agree with J. Gresham Machen when he says of the word orthodox, "A thing is 'orthodox' if it is in accordance with the Bible. I think we might well revive the word. But whether we revive the word or not, we certainly ought to hold to the thing that is designated by the word." For now it seems that reformed has the lion's share.

[42] For an excellent argument on avoiding criticism and pointless arguments yet pursuing theological truth and debate read "On Controversy" by John Newton. Ligonier Ministries. Accessed July 27, 2024.
https://www.ligonier.org/learn/articles/on-controversy

[43] To state it as strongly as I can, a wrong understanding of scripture is nothing

less than idolatry. AW Tozer cautioned, "Let us beware lest we in our pride accept the erroneous notion that idolatry consists only in kneeling before visible objects of adoration and that civilized peoples are therefore free from it. The essence of idolatry is the entertainment of thoughts about God that are unworthy of Him. It begins in the mind and may be present where no overt act of worship has taken place."

[44] For a more thorough investigation into the weightier and lighter elements of doctrine, I recommend Albert Mohler's concept of Theological Triage, A Call for Theological Triage and Christian Maturity - AlbertMohler.com. Accessed July 27, 2024. https://albertmohler.com/2005/07/12/a-call-for-theological-triage-and-christian-maturity/

[45] Before going further, it is necessary to address the most common critique against doctrine: that we cannot be sure; therefore, we should not divide among it. This, however, is a denial that God has revealed himself plainly and in language we can understand; as JI Packer illustrates, "If there are problems in grasping [revealed truth], the problems are in us, not in scripture." Scripture was not given to confuse, mislead, or equivocate it was given that we may understand. To be sure, there are areas in the Bible that allow for freedom in Christ, and we "major on the majors and minor on the minors" in response, especially in the therapeutic relationship.

[46] J. Gresham Machen said, "But if any one fact is clear, on the basis of this evidence, it is that the Christian movement at its inception was not just a way of life in the modern sense, but a way of life founded upon a message. It was based, not upon mere feeling, not upon a mere program of work, but upon an account of facts. In other words it was based upon doctrine."

Machen JG. *Christianity and Liberalism*. Macmillan; 1923.

[47] AW Tozer wrote, "Creedal truth is a coal lying inert in the depths of the earth awaiting release. Dig it out, shovel it into a combustion chamber of some huge engine, and the mighty energy that lay asleep for centuries will create light and head and cause the machinery of a great factory to surge into production again. The theory of coal never turned a wheel nor warmed a hearth. Power must be released to be made effective."

Tozer AW. *The Radical Cross: Living the Passion of Christ*. Reissue edition. Moody Publishers; 2015.

[48] The social revolution and civil rights that the Christian gospel initiated, of

which some were lost before the reformation, cannot be understated from breaking of social class, care for the poor, widowed, orphaned, sanctity of human life, condemnation of slavery, among others. I recommend:

Holland T. *Dominion: How the Christian Revolution Remade the World*. Basic Books; 2019.

[49] O'Neill A. *The Mind after Eden: Psychiatry in a Post-Fall World*. Independently published; 2022.

[50] *Westminster Confession of Faith*. Fig; 2010. Chapter 3.1

[51] Dittmann M. What makes good people do bad things? *Monitor on Psychology*. October 2004;35(9):68.

[52] Time does not permit us to discuss the spectrum of evil humans are capable of, which includes a spectrum from dozens of dictators, war crimes, and abuses to the obstinate and selfish attitudes displayed by toddlers.
[53] Kelley T "Stricken, Smitten, and Afflicted." (1769-1854). Public Domain.
[54] Carnegie D. *How to Win Friends and Influence People*. Sristhi Publishers & Distributors; 2020.

[55] Cowper W. "Praise for the Fountain Opened." 1772. Public Domain.
[56] Gibson J. Limited Atonement. *Tabletalk Magazine*, April 2019.
[57] Scrupulosity OCD is a common presentation of the disorder, for more information see my chapter on OCD in:

O'Neill A. *The Mind after Eden: Psychiatry in a Post-Fall World*. Independently published; 2022.

[58] Bunyan J. *Grace Abounding to the Chief of Sinners: Or, A Brief and Faithful Relation of the Exceeding Mercy of God in Christ, to His Poor Servant John Bunyan*. Ginn; 1910.

[59] The soul that is against God does not in any way naturally incline toward God, it instead causes us to hide from his presence and cover ourselves as Adam and Eve did in the Garden. We reject his grace, not draw toward in our fallen state. (Gen. 3:10)
[60] Westminster Shorter Catechism, Question 1.
[61] Much like: Powlison D. Affirmations and Denials. *JBC*. 19:1. 2000.
[62] For a greater exploration of how we arrived at this philosophy, see:

Trueman CR. *Strange New World: How Thinkers and Activists Redefined Identity and Sparked the Sexual Revolution*. Crossway; 2022.

[63] C.S. Lewis defined this term as "the uncritical acceptance of the intellectual climate of our own age and the assumption that whatever has gone out of date is on that count discredited."

[64] The text of this sermon can be found in my book:

O'Neill A. *The Patience of Hope: Encouragement for the Sufferer through the Life and Preaching of George Matheson*. Adam O'Neill & Associates LLC; 2024.

[65] Elliot E. *The Path of Loneliness: Finding Your Way through the Wilderness to God*. Baker Publishing Group; 2024.

[66] Joni Eareckson-Tada: A Bruised Reed - YouTube. Accessed July 27, 2024. https://www.youtube.com/watch?v=WaMfU4h3VX0&t=2642s&ab_channel=LigonierMinistries

[67] Nietzsche's concept of Übermensch in Nietzsche F. *Thus Spoke Zarathustra: A Book for Everyone and Nobody*. Oxford University Press; 2008.

Übermensch: literally over-human, sometimes translated as super-man, calls forth a person who makes their own values, overcomes suffering, and whose life is not dictated by the teachings of the church. Nietzsche's concept of the superman would be incompatible with the life of Jesus.

[68] I believe it is important to define suffering, especially when examining one's life. My preferred definition of suffering comes from Elisabeth Elliot: "Having what you don't want or wanting what you don't have."

[69] See the *Doctor Angelicus* St. Thomas Aquinas' *Summa Theologica*, (ST I, q50). Thomas (Aquinas) S. *The "Summa Theologica" of St. Thomas Aquinas*. R. & T. Washbourne; 1922.

[70] Latin: "Before the sight of God".

[71] Ortlund D. *Gentle and Lowly: The Heart of Christ for Sinners and Sufferers*. Crossway; 2020. pg 97.

[72] Ibid. pg. 138.

[73] Keller T, Keller K. *The Meaning of Marriage: Facing the Complexities of Commitment with the Wisdom of God*. Reprint edition. Penguin Books; 2013.

[74] Ortlund D. *Deeper: Real Change for Real Sinners*. Crossway; 2021.

If it were not unethical and an evidence of wild laziness, I would copy and paste the entirety of Ortlund's book at the end of this chapter leading into the next. I am in complete agreement that the path of sanctification lies principally on the road of a greater knowledge of our justification.

[75] As R.C. Sproul frequently said, the saying of Jesus can be hard in that they are (1) hard to understand or (2) hard to hear. Both caused followers of Jesus to turn away. See sermon series: The Hard Sayings of Jesus by R.C. Sproul | Ligonier Ministries. Accessed July 27, 2024. https://www.ligonier.org/learn/series/hard-sayings-of-jesus

[76] Though ironically it is Christians who frequently find themselves in physical chains, it is only the Christian, as evidenced by Paul's frequent imprisonment, that can truly rejoice to know the freedom which Jesus secured far supersedes that of physical restraints and dives as deep into the soul as freedom from the law and from sin and death.

[77] Chalmers T. *The Expulsive Power of a New Affection. A Sermon.* Hatchard&Company; 1861.

[78] Bavinck H, Wynne RC. *The Wonderful Works of God.* First Edition. Westminster Seminary Press; 2020. pg. 286.

[79] Tozer AW. *The Radical Cross: Living the Passion of Christ.* Reissue edition. Moody Publishers; 2015. Pg. 102.

[80] Michael Reeves: The Triunity of God - YouTube. Accessed July 27, 2024. https://www.youtube.com/watch?v=xTrfb9tJzp4&ab_channel=LigonierMinistries. Sermon Audio Transcription.

[81] Bavinck H, Wynne RC. *The Wonderful Works of God.* First Edition. Westminster Seminary Press; 2020. pg. 328.

[82] Dever M. *What Is a Healthy Church?* Crossway; 2007. pg. 29.

[83] "Spiritual Gifts". Audio. John Piper, March 15, 1981.

[84] …though be careful, God often calls us to areas of perceived weakness because it is precisely here where he shows His strength in your gifting. Perceived weakness, however, is not the same as actual weakness in an area. For example, I am grateful my Christian brothers and sisters are gifted with interacting with children. I don't just have a perceived weakness in this area, I actually struggle, consistently. I ask children too young to understand about the planets and children to old about colors. Both of us end up embarrassed. Praise God for the Body which has hands and feet.

[85] The name of the capital of Hell in John Milton's epic poem *Paradise Lost*. A fitting description of life without the Holy Spirit and His fruit.

[86] Though debated, some have described this as part of the "eyes being opened" in Genesis 3:7, which leads to a "knowing." Gone was the child-like innocence and obedience they displayed prior to the fall. Before The Fall, Adam and Eve enjoyed a relationship of complete trust in God. The past unfolded, as far as they were

concerned, exactly as it should; the future was left in the faithful hands of their Creator God. I am not suggesting that the frontal lobe is the evidence of The Fall, for there is much to give great thanks for in its complex functions, rather that the power of such a brain section was morphed by sin into a thorn that plagues us to this day.

[87] Paul Washer said, "If salvation was 99.99% Jesus and 0.01% us, we would all be damned". Because God's saving and sustaining grace are not different but come from the same source, Him, we can trust He has provided the necessary grace to accomplish His perfect will in our lives.

[88] Boom C ten, Sherrill E, Sherrill J. *The Hiding Place*. Chosen Books; 2015.

[89] Sproul RC. *Chosen By God: Know God's Perfect Plan for His Glory and His Children*. Tyndale House Publishers; 1986.

[90] Romans 11:36

[91] Nouwen H. *Turn My Mourning into Dancing: Finding Hope in Hard Times*. Thomas Nelson; 2004.

[92] Tessa Thompson in her article "Walking Through Trials, Temptations, and Tests" *Tabletalk* writes, "…this is the pattern we see throughout the New Testament Epistles. In all their concerns about the present, the writers were ultimately aiming at Christ's return, creation's renewal, and the believer's glorification. Every Command, every encouragement from the gospel, every rebuke and affirmation, every explanation of God's character and ways—in all these things, the end goal is not a happy Christian life on earth but a coming, eternal life with Christ in heaven."

Thompson. Walking through Trials, Temptations, and Tests. *Tabletalk*. Published online August 1, 2023. Accessed July 27, 2024. https://tabletalkmagazine.com/article/2023/08/walking-through-trials-temptations-and-tests/

[93] I should note that throwing medication away in common trash is not advisable (nor is flushing it down the toilet); it can pollute our water, be more easily accessible to children, or be found and used by someone along the trash disposal process. Instead, many pharmacies and police stations have drop-offs where specialized chemicals deactivate the active medication, making them safe for normal disposal.

[94] This is a purposeful nod to John Piper's now famous sermon in Memphis, known colloquially as the "Seashell Sermon," which is worth listening to in its entirety on DesiringGod.org. In it, Piper pleads with us to "not waste our lives."

[95] I am often asked if it is not a good idea for a Christian to see a non-Christian provider. I respond that what concerns me is not a Christian seeing a non-Christian (for discernment will help them tell the truth from error) but instead, we

should fear a non-Christian seeing a non-Christian. It is in that relationship that pure relief of pain, secular humanism, and moral relativism, among many other destructive worldviews, guide treatment, and neither provider nor patient can see it clearly.

[96] As Sinclair Ferguson said in his sermon "Adam and Christ,": "The Luster of the work of Jesus Christ shines so brightly when we realize the catastrophe that our first father, Adam, created for all men." He likens it to a jeweler placing a sparkling diamond atop a black velvet cloth.

[97] I can hear my Swedish great-grandmother saying to me when I was young, "Only one life, 'twill soon be past, Only what's done for Christ will last." C.T. Studd.

[98] Goodwin DD T. *The Heart of Christ in Heaven towards Sinners on Earth.*; 1645. pg. 155-156.

[99] Kings Kaleidoscope. "All Glory Be To Christ." (2013). Hymn.

[100] Gregory RL. Seeing after blindness. *Nat Neurosci.* 2003;6(9):909-910. doi:10.1038/nn0903-909

[101] I feel, like Martin Luther, that "We must make a great difference between God's Word and the word of man. A man's word is a little sound, that flies into the air, and soon vanishes; but the Word of God is greater than heaven and earth, yea, greater than death and hell, for it forms part of the power of God, and endures everlastingly."

[102] Trinitarian theology and psychology: the fact that this topic is written in a footnote is not a statement on the depth or worth of the topic; quite the opposite. An exploration into the full implications of Trinitarian theology on psychology is beyond the scope of this book if we desire to investigate it entirely, but it is not irrelevant, so it bears introducing here. Though there is much that could be said, suffice to say now, our God-glorifying orientation of psychology is rooted in Trinitarian theology. Our three aims of knowledge, conformity, and effectiveness mirror the actions and intentions of the three persons of the Godhead. The Father, who's Divine will is progressively revealed and our relationship to Him is one like Christ to the Father. To know Him, know His will, and how He has ordered the world as Christ grew in wisdom and statue, and favor with God and man (Luke 2:52)—the first aim. Then as Christ was obedient in all things, we strive to become like him, conforming into obedience to the Father's will (John 5:19)—the second aim. This is accomplished through the Holy Spirit, who provides the effectual power and accomplishes the gospel's work on the earth (Luke 24:49)—the third aim. Lord willing, this concept will be explored in depth in another book.

Made in the USA
Middletown, DE
18 May 2025